D1213901

350

The
Five-Hundred-Word
Theme

LEE J. MARTIN
*Texas A & M
University*

The
Five-Hundred-Word
Theme

Prentice-Hall, Inc.
Englewood Cliffs, N.J.

© 1968, by
PRENTICE-HALL, INC.
Englewood Cliffs, N.J.

All rights reserved. No part of this book
may be reproduced in any form or by any
means without permission in writing from
the publisher.

Library of Congress Catalog Card No.: 68-16527

Current printing *(last number)* :
10   9   8   7

Printed in the United States of America

PRENTICE-HALL INTERNATIONAL, INC., *London*

PRENTICE-HALL OF AUSTRALIA, PTY. LTD., *Sydney*

PRENTICE-HALL OF CANADA, LTD., *Toronto*

PRENTICE-HALL OF INDIA PRIVATE LTD., *New Delhi*

PRENTICE-HALL OF JAPAN, INC., *Tokyo*

Preface

This book offers the freshman composition student the basic knowledge necessary to write a short theme of the type most often required in beginning composition courses. I have made two assumptions: that most students will profit little in college by further formal study of "mechanics" of the language, and that students need above all an orderly approach to the problem of organizing and writing a short paper that makes a logical point and supports it. Such an orderly approach is the subject of this book. The student is not burdened with the trivia of mechanics.

I have used the five-hundred-word theme, because in this length a student can best learn and practice the principles that apply to all writing. Never do I intend to imply, however, that themes assigned should be exactly five hundred words. I do intend that they should be close to this length. A shorter paper gives the student little opportunity to develop his subject; a longer one becomes burdensome for both student and teacher without offering any particular advantage to the beginning writer.

I have stressed organization. Indeed, the diagrams in the book present a pattern for organizing the short theme—a pattern for the beginning student to follow one step at a time until he has learned and practiced the basic principles of composition. I have purposely forced the student into a mold to minimize the mysteries of writing expository prose and to teach him to support his ideas as logically as possible. I would not expect him to stay in the mold after his first semester of college composition, but I would expect him to apply the principles taught here to all his writing.

I am deeply indebted to my wife Harriet, who supplied a number of the exercises and offered invaluable editorial help. My thanks also go to Sterling Swift, Jim Campbell, and Paul O'Connell of Prentice-Hall, and to Professor Gary Tate, The University of Tulsa, Professor Donald J. Tighe, St. Petersburg Junior College, and Professor John R. Willingham, The University of Kansas, who read the manuscript and offered helpful criticism.

The student essays included for analysis were contributed by former students of mine. I express my appreciation to Maxine Batts, Eleanor Bostick, Gerald Ellison, Jerry Griffiths, Dorthea Robinson, William Swindle, Doris Thompson, Carey Lee White, and Louise Ward.

L.J.M.

Contents

1 Seeing the Whole Paper   1

INTRODUCTION   *1*
What Learning to Write Better Can Do for You,   1
What You Must Bring to Writing,   2
What You Are Expected to Do,   3
ORGANIZING THE PAPER   *4*
                Exercises, 11

2 Getting Started   19

Choosing a Subject,   19
Limiting Your Subject,   21
Framing Your Thesis Statement,   23
             Exercises, 31
Stating Your Purpose,   32
             Exercises, 35

3 Maintaining Unity and Coherence   37

UNITY   *37*
             Exercises, 45

COHERENCE   *48*
Consistent Point of View,   49
Chronological Order of Sentences,   50
Repetition of Key Words,   51
Spatial Order of Sentences,   52
Related Sentence Patterns,   54
Pronoun Reference,   55
Transition Words,   56
             Exercises, 59

4 Writing Paragraphs 65

INTRODUCTORY PARAGRAPH 65
DEVELOPMENTAL PARAGRAPHS 66
Exercises, 72

Using Specific Detail, 73
Exercises, 74

Using Details in Paragraph Development, 75
Summary, 79
Exercises, 80

DEVELOPMENT BY USE OF DEFINITION 81
Classification, 83
Synonym, 86
Example of Illustration, 86
Enumeration, 86
Function (Operational Definition), 87
Exercises, 88

Extended Definition, 88
Exercises, 90

*PARAGRAPH DEVELOPMENT BY USE OF
ILLUSTRATION* 91
Exercises, 95

*DEVELOPMENT BY USE OF COMPARISON OR
CONTRAST* 96
Exercises, 99

DEVELOPMENT BY REASONS 99
Exercises, 102

*METHODS OF DEVELOPMENT IN
COMBINATION* 103

5 Putting the Parts Together: The Whole Paper 105

Writing Assignment, 116

6 Revising Your Paper—Diction 118

Change the Passive Voice to Active Voice, 118
Exercise, 121

Avoid Listless Verbs, 122
            Exercise, 123

Examine All Uses of "Who" and "Which," 124
            Exercise, 126

Avoid Anything Trite, 127
Or Any Exhausted Phrase, 128
            Exercises, 128

Avoid Forcing Your Reader to Love It, 129
Do Not Preach, 130
Avoid Stilted Wording, 131
            Exercise, 131

Avoid "Fine Writing," 132
Avoid "ly" Words, 132
Avoid Vague Words, 133
            Review Exercises, 134

7 Revising Your Paper—Sentences   136

THE SIMPLE SENTENCE   136
            Exercise, 139

Emphasizing Words and Ideas in a Sentence, 139
The Periodic Sentence, 141
The Loose Sentence, 142
The Periodic-Loose Sentence, 145
            Exercise, 145

SECONDARY SENTENCE PATTERNS:
COORDINATION AND SUBORDINATION   146
Coordination, 147
Punctuation of Coordinate Elements, 148
            Exercises, 149

Coordinate Elements in Series, 150
            Exercise, 154

SUBORDINATION   155
            Exercise, 157

SUMMARY EXERCISES   158

Seeing the Whole Paper

1

I. INTRODUCTION

Writing, like any human skill, can be taught in principle and perfected by practice. This book is designed to teach you the basic principles you need to write a five-hundred-word paper—the same principles involved in any writing—and it will give you practice in applying these principles when you work the exercises in each chapter. It will introduce the parts of the five-hundred-word paper one at a time and allow you to practice each before proceeding to the next. Then this book will direct you in putting all the parts together into a paper, and finally, it will furnish a guide to revising the paper.

What Learning to Write Better Can Do for You

The most obvious advantage of improving your writing is being able to put your ideas into understandable and valid form. Many students have good ideas, but they do not know how to express them, either in writing or speaking. Composing a paper is one way you can learn to state your ideas specifically and to show the evidence you have to support those ideas. Unless you write down ideas, however, they are likely to remain half-formed, and when you attempt to express them, you may find that you are not successful in communicating specifically what you mean. Suppose, for example, that your best friend has decided to run for a class office and that you think he has the qualities of an outstanding class officer. Further suppose that he asks you, as his closest friend, to present these qualities to the student body by writing a letter to the college newspaper. How would you go about explaining these qualities so that the readers of the newspaper would believe in your friend as you do? The study and practice of the techniques of expository writing will, in the long run, make it second nature for you to be able to express and support your ideas clearly and concisely in any situation.

Having the skill of communication at your command will help you to gain confidence in your own ability to function as an individual—one capable of carrying his own weight in any social or business situation. Suppose, again, that you have decided to try to

1

get a job next summer in one of our national parks or in a summer camp as a counselor for youngsters. It would be necessary for you to write a letter outlining all your qualifications to hold this job. You would have to sell yourself to the person doing the hiring. And you can do this well only if you have the confidence of knowing how to arrange your credentials so that you will be presented in the best possible manner to your prospective employer. Similarly, in your school work, a knowledge of the techniques of expository writing will greatly increase your chances for a better grade in any course. Any essay examination that confronts you or any paper that you must write requires the application of a knowledge of the organization of ideas, and the more effectively you present to your teachers the ideas and knowledge you have, the more your writing will improve and the better your grade will be on that piece of writing.

Perhaps most important to you, however, as a young citizen of our democracy, is the ability to write logically and recognize logical thought when you read it or hear it. Practicing the techniques of expository writing makes it necessary for you to use all the evidence you can collect to support the ideas you want your reader to accept. As you collect evidence, you cannot help becoming aware of the logic of your ideas. If the evidence disproves your ideas, then discard them. But if your evidence indicates that you are probably right, you are justified in presenting and supporting your ideas. In the same way, if you know how much evidence it takes to support a generalization, you will be more cautious in accepting what you hear or read, unless valid supporting evidence is offered. Such a cautious approach to an idea, sometimes called skepticism, is necessary for the survival of a democracy: No one person or group can lead the entire nation down the wrong path as long as proof is demanded to support ideas. Indeed, open debate, the clash of ideas and their proof, has always been fundamental in developing our country.

What You Must Bring to Writing

You must first realize that good writing is not easy. It demands patience and discipline. Do not expect to sit down and produce a successful paper in the time it takes you to write down the words. Some writers with much experience might be able to do this, for their very experience enables them to choose the proper word and to frame their sentences exactly; but most established writers find writing laborious. Certainly the rest of us do, if we attempt to turn out work that we can be proud of and that will communicate precisely what we intend. Good writing also requires self-discipline. You must learn to cast your paragraphs in forms that convey your intention and give the writing unity and coherence. You must learn economy in wording, and you must learn to stick with a single, limited subject so that you finish with a definite pre-established point that has been developed and supported. You must discipline yourself to think through your subject thoroughly before you write the first word.

The thought you bring to writing is of utmost importance. Without it you cannot write at all, for writing *is* the communication of thought. You must think through your subject before starting to write, and you must write with logical thought. You may, for instance, have to discard some of your prejudices—those ideas and opinions you hold without logic and evidence to back them up—because they are based in emotion rather than in fact. Have you, for instance, ever really examined the *facts* about your college, your town, or your state, and compared them to the facts about other schools, towns, or states in order to develop a mature attitude toward "home"? Or do you automatically defend them, blindly and emotionally, without looking at the facts? Everyone thinks irrationally at times, but the irrational has no place in writing. You must have an open and inquiring mind, as free from prejudice and unfounded opinion as you can make it, so that you can accept fact where you find it and can develop the habit of accepting only fact in support of generalizations.

You must, then, have the desire to become educated. You must want to be able to face fact without coloring or slanting it to fit a set of prejudices, to communicate soundly supported ideas to others either in speech or writing, to lose any narrow provincialism, and to consider ideas that do not necessarily concern only restricted interests. Then can you become mature and educated, and learning the techniques of effective communication in writing will hasten the process.

What You Are Expected to Do

Expository writing is the concern of this book, so it should be defined. *Exposition* is one of the four principal types of prose, the other three being *argumentation*, *narration*, and *description*. Primarily, expository writing concerns itself with explaining an idea, an object, or a process. If, for instance, you want to establish the idea that the organization of social clubs on your campus would benefit the students, you would be writing exposition, that is, you would be explaining your idea. Or if you want to explain the difficulties involved in following a dress pattern or making a cake or building a hot-rod, you would be using *exposition*. If, on the other hand, you attempt to prove that social clubs should be outlawed on your campus, you would be using *argumentation*. If you give an account of how something happened, you are using *narration*; and if you describe how something looks, feels, tastes, or what it sounds or smells like, you are using *description*. In ordinary writing, these types are not always used separately; two or more of the types might be mixed in a single essay. Argumentation is commonly used to reinforce explanation, or description is blended with exposition. Any writing—no matter what combination of types is used—that has as its primary purpose *to make a subject clear* we will consider expository writing.

Your writing, for the purposes of this book, will consist chiefly of papers of approximately five hundred words as well as single paragraphs of more than one hundred words. The writing of single paragraphs is required to give you practice in the discipline and skill of using the various means of developing paragraphs clearly. They are never written as ends in themselves but only as parts of clearly organized and well-developed papers. If you follow the principles set down in this book, carefully examining the illustrations, you should be able to compose acceptably this clearly organized and well-developed paper of five-hundred words. Because the principles of good expository writing apply to any writing situation, whether it be a scientific report or a letter to a friend, these principles will aid you in all that you do.

II. ORGANIZING THE PAPER

Before starting to write anything, you need a specific idea of what you are supposed to produce. Your product, a five-hundred-word paper, can be schematically diagrammed to show it as a whole and to indicate the relationship of each part of the paper to the other parts. This is such a diagram. Examine it.

Each block in the diagram represents one paragraph of the five-hundred-word paper. The first block shows the introductory paragraph. The line across the bottom stands for the final sentence in that paragraph: This is the thesis statement for your paper, the one main point that your paper will develop and support. This position for the thesis statement is an arbitrary one; it does not have to come in this position. It can appear at the beginning of the intro-

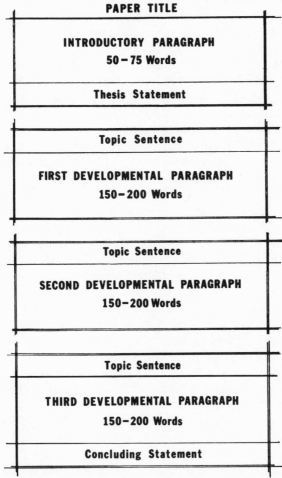

PAPER TITLE

INTRODUCTORY PARAGRAPH
50 – 75 Words

Thesis Statement

Topic Sentence

FIRST DEVELOPMENTAL PARAGRAPH
150 – 200 Words

Topic Sentence

SECOND DEVELOPMENTAL PARAGRAPH
150 – 200 Words

Topic Sentence

THIRD DEVELOPMENTAL PARAGRAPH
150 – 200 Words

Concluding Statement

ductory paragraph or at the end of the whole paper. Or it does not have to be stated at all; it can be implied so that the reader must determine for himself beyond any doubt the logical point your evidence supports. Until you are sure of yourself in framing a thesis statement, it is better to put the thesis at the end of the introductory paragraph for several reasons: It allows the reader to catch his breath while the writer establishes common ground; it keeps the writer from confusing the reader by putting information that may appear to be narrowing the subject between the thesis statement and the first paragraph of the body; and it facilitates coherence by putting the thesis statement close to the body of the paper.

The position of the thesis statement determines the method of organization to be used. If you give evidence for your thesis first and then end the paper with a specific or implied statement of the thesis, you are using the *inductive* method. However, if you give the thesis first, as recommended here, and then follow it with supporting evidence, the method is *deductive*. The beginning writer is safer with the deductive method. The skilled organizer tries other methods and becomes more creative.

In the block representing the paper's second paragraph, labeled First Developmental Paragraph, the first sentence is the topic sentence. Again, this position is arbitrary. The topic sentence can come in the middle, or at the end, of the paragraph, or it can be implied. But for the first few papers you write, place all topic sentences, specifically stated, at the beginning of paragraphs. The topic sentence is for the paragraph what the thesis statement is for the whole paper, that is, it is the one point the paragraph makes. But it is even more closely related to the thesis statement; it is one reason the thesis statement is valid. The remainder of the paragraph, about 150 to 200 words, is evidence put forth to establish the soundness of the topic sentence. So when this paragraph is written, there will be one tightly reasoned unit supporting the main point of the paper. You will have two more such units in the paper.

The topic sentence in the Second Developmental Paragraph is the second "proof" of the thesis, or main point, and the material presented in the paragraph supports this second topic sentence. When you have completed this paragraph, support of the thesis statement becomes much stronger. You have given two reasons to show that the thesis statement is valid, and you have supported each of those reasons with logical evidence to prove their validity.

The final paragraph, the Third Developmental Paragraph, should be the strongest in support of the thesis statement. Put the most important reason—the one you think will clinch the point—as the topic sentence of this paragraph. Give it strong support in the remainder of the paragraph, and you will leave the reader with the conviction that you are right. Once you have him at this point, hit him with the concluding statement as the last sentence in the whole paper. The concluding statement simply restates the thesis statement so that you finish by reminding the reader that this is the point you have made in the paper. It is better not to make the point in the exact words used at the beginning of the paper, so somewhat change the wording and it will have a greater effect on the reader, particularly because it concludes your strongest paragraph.

Do not under any circumstances tell the reader that you are ending your paper. Such statements as "In conclusion it can be seen that. . . ." or "To sum up. . . ." are trite and unnecessary. Neither is a formal concluding paragraph necessary. In a much longer paper, summing up is often desirable; but in a five-hundred-word paper, the concluding statement does the necessary summing up, and you and the reader are spared the tediousness and triteness of a bloated concluding paragraph that adds nothing to the paper.

This diagram represents a convenient pattern for writing the five-hundred-word paper. But it is just that—a formula, a recipe. If your subject requires variation, then alter it; add or delete a paragraph. You will know how because you will have learned the basic pattern. But until you do learn the pattern, follow the diagram you have just studied. The freshman student who wrote the paper below followed it exactly (the thesis statement, topic sentences, and concluding statement are italicized).

THE ABUSIVE SOCIAL FRATERNITIES

At many colleges and universities—particularly among those in the South—the social fraternity, not the classroom, is the chief concern of the student body. *These social fraternities are undesirable in American universities* because they are expensive, they deter academic achievement, and they are undemocratic.

When a college student pledges as a member of a fraternity, *he burdens himself with exorbitant expenses that are not incurred by the nonfraternity student.* The first expense the pledge must face is the initiation fee, which normally amounts to about seventy-five dollars. In addition to buying his fraternity membership, he must pay annual dues, the cost of which varies among the brotherhoods. To be able to enjoy the fellowship of his fraternity brothers, the student must live in the house belonging to the local chapter. Here room and board will cost about eighty-five dollars a month, but the student living in university housing will pay only fifty-five dollars a month. The fraternity brother is also assessed a certain amount to finance all chapter-sponsored events, no matter whether he plans to attend those activities.

Although fraternity expenses are less of a detriment to the richer members, *the society interferes indiscriminately with the studies of each of its members.* Students are required to attend various social events that proscribe evening study, and many chapters require each member to have a specified number of dates each week. In addition to attending the required social activities, each fraternity member is assigned certain time-consuming responsibilities. Whereas an older fraternity brother may be a chapter officer or a member of one of various chapter committees, the pledge normally is forced to do menial tasks or personal services. It may be his duty to help clean the chapter house, or he may be responsible for shining shoes, pressing clothes, washing cars, or running errands for the older brothers. In the fraternity house where education becomes an extracurricular activity, there prevails a social rather than an academic atmosphere.

But a scholastic atmosphere inbued with freedom of thought cannot exist in a social order lacking in democracy. With admission requirements discriminating against minority groups such as Negroes, Orientals, or Jews as well as against undesirable Anglo-Saxons, the college fraternity thrives on exclusiveness. Where eligibility is concerned, merit is no matter. Monied ancestry is of far greater consequence than character and individual worth. WHO the pledge is, not WHAT he is, counts, and the one whose great-uncle chartered the chapter is sure to shine. Discrimination combined with limited memberships produces a social order that perpetuates a supposedly elite blood line and a caste system in which pride in membership is inevitable. *As a result, there have been established on college campuses hollow, vain aristocracies that have no place in academic communities.*

Note that this paper makes one main point, social fraternities are undesirable in American universities, and each topic sentence offers one reason for the validity of the main point. The first topic sentence, italicized in the second paragraph, makes the point that fraternities are undesirable *because* they cost too much. The remainder of the paragraph establishes this topic sentence as valid by pointing out the expense of belonging to a fraternity. It lists the initiation fee, the annual dues, room and board, and special assessments for social events. The second topic sentence, italicized in the third paragraph, points out that fraternities are undesirable *because* they do not allow members enough time for study. In support of this topic sentence, the remainder of the paragraph lists required social events and dates, committee membership, chapter offices, and especially for the pledge, time-consuming menial tasks such as cleaning house, shining shoes, washing cars, and running errands. The third topic sentence, italicized at the beginning of the fourth paragraph, advances what the writer considers his strongest reason in support of the thesis statement—that fraternities are undesirable *because* they are undemocratic. The remainder of the paragraph supports this topic sentence by pointing to discrimination against minority groups, to selection of pledges for money and family, and to limited memberships. These, it asserts, lead to belief in elite blood lines and caste systems. The concluding statement, italicized

PAPER TITLE

INTRODUCTORY PARAGRAPH
50 — 75 words.

Thesis Statement: Social fraternities are undesirable in American Universities.

Topic Sentence 1: Fraternity members are burdened with exorbitant expenses.

Support for Topic Sentence 1
A. Initiation fees are high.
B. Annual dues are costly.
C. Living expenses in the house are higher than those in university housing.
D. Chapter-sponsored events must be financed by members.

FIRST DEVELOPMENTAL PARAGRAPH
150-200 words.

Topic Sentence 2: Social fraternities interfere with the study of its members.

Support for Topic Sentence 2
A. Compulsory social events consume study time.
B. Members are assigned time-consuming responsibilities in the chapter

SECOND DEVELOPMENTAL PARAGRAPH
150-200 words.

Topic Sentence 3: Social fraternities lack democracy.

Support for Topic Sentence 3
A. Admission requirements discriminate against minority groups.
B. Prospective pledges' merit counts less than background.
C. Pride in "blood line" and a caste system is maintained.

Concluding Statement: Social fraternities—vain, hollow aristocracies—have no place in academic communities.

THIRD DEVELOPMENTAL PARAGRAPH
150-200 words.

at the end of the fourth paragraph, restates the thesis and sums up the paper. Although this paper needs revisions before it is a finished product, the writer has made his point and supported it as well as he can from evidence based on his own experience and observation.

The organization of the five-hundred-word paper can be shown in another type of diagram. This one inserts the supporting points for each topic sentence. (See page nine.)

With this framework of thesis statement, three reasons to uphold the thesis statement, support for the reasons, and a concluding statement, you could have written the five-hundred-word paper on the evils of social fraternities. Now read the paper below and determine whether it is a better paper than the one on fraternities.

THE PRACTICAL COLLEGE MARRIAGE

Two really can live as cheaply as one, but as any struggling coed and her haunted husband can testify, those two had better prepare for a painful existence, but *practical*. The money that the folks were glad to send their young one must now serve two. The lessons this pair learns are the most practical in the world, though. They know before the honeymoon is over that, although they'll cry a lot, they'll learn to slice their output and savor their income. They learn to be practical about entertainment, about the care and mending of garments, and about the nourishing qualities of peanut butter.

Entertainment is not what it used to be. In the old days, Mary took for granted two or three movies a week and dancing at least on Saturday night. Mom and Dad didn't mind paying that little bit, as long as their college daughter kept up her grades. Now in their room-with-kitchen-privileges apartment Mary and Jim get along fine —but movies are out, and they wouldn't dream of trying to squeeze a dancing cover charge out of what little Dad sends and Jim can earn. For entertainment, Jim can help with the dishes, and they can walk together, hand in hand, to the library for a blissful evening of research. It's a terribly *practical* pursuit, actually.

The clothing situation gets serious. Neither Mary nor her Jim would dare gain weight, even if their home-cooked meals were that tempting. They dressed well in their single days, and they still do, but alas, in the very same garments that looked so much better last semester. Shoes get resoled now, instead of replaced, and the shine on Jim's "good" suit is more noticeable. It isn't as though he had to keep up with his fraternity brothers any longer. Camaraderie with that carefree group is nice to remember, but meeting with the boys is no longer practical. Mary watches fashions, but she does not buy the fads. She found out in a hurry that it is not the *practical* way to dress.

Their menu does not vary much, and there is no longer the balanced touch of the dormitory dietician. They watch out for yellow and green vegetables, of course, and a potato a day with some kind of protein. But the old zip is gone, and with it went between-class cokes and Sunday at the Garden Steakhouse with the rest of the English majors. They are grateful, naturally, to the famous scientist who developed peanut butter. Even if it does stick to the palate and begin to grow old too soon, Mary and Jim buy more peanut butter, because it's so very *practical*. But when it's all over and the children are grown, Jim and Mary will look back on these days as some of the best in their lives, because look at the great lessons they learned.

Check back over the diagram for the five-hundred-word paper, and you will see that this paper follows the diagram exactly but notice that it is not a slavish line-by-line copy of it. There is plenty of creativity in translating the diagram into the paper—in diction, in sentence structure, in expression of ideas. It is not necessary to write a stilted, formal paper just because you are writing from an outline. Put your own personality into what you write by the way you express yourself to your reader. When you do this, you let the reader see your feelings, and your paper will not be dull, whatever else it may be.

EXERCISES

I. Analyze the following papers for organization. Answer the questions at the end of each paper to aid your analysis.

A. MISPLACED GOALS IN EDUCATION STIFLE THE INQUIRING MIND

1. Lack of encouragement of creativity in the present school system discourages a real search for knowledge. Importance continually placed on following a certain form has given the student a misplaced set of values.

2. Even though following directions is important, too often a pupil is graded solely on how well he does this. In spite of his original thought, his grade may be low because he left too small a margin, he wrote on the bottom line, or he numbered the pages in the wrong corner. Following a rigid form of Roman numerals, the student loses sight of the content of the material. If he has researched the subject, he might lose all credit because he has not tagged his sources properly. Emphasis should be placed on the thought shown in his work rather than on rigid adherence to a given form.

3. Thinking things through for himself, the student might come up with an idea other than his professor's. Grade school and high school have taught him that this is not advisable. The student who can most nearly duplicate the teacher's instruction is regarded most highly. If the teacher will "lay it on

the line," then it can be easily duplicated. Such narrow goals restrict the student, making him conform to the ideas already set out for him. Stepping outside the expected way of working a problem, finding a different meaning to a passage in literature, or bringing some original idea to class is penalized.

4. Memorization of details clutters the mind with facts that are never assimilated. World geography consists of a detailed compilation of isolated facts on individual countries. "How many square miles is Uraguay?" and "What is its population?" are asked rather than "How has its location in South America affected its economic growth?" The value of associating the past with the future is lost in history classes where twenty dates are given—the student is asked to write who was president and vice-president.

5. With elementary and secondary education goals set on teaching students to follow strict forms or to reproduce an instructor's or text's words and memorize details without connecting them, it is easily understandable that students today apparently lack an inquiring mind. Any deviation from the usual they wish to do must be done outside their classwork.

6. To encourage original thought educational goals must be realigned. Importance must be placed on the entire content of the material and its broad implications. Reslanting history to increase the value, using geography in studies of modern economics and politics, looking into physics proofs rather than just formulas will help stimulate thought. A broadening of teachers' views will broaden the scope and responsibility of the student. More scholastic freedom and more creative goals will reawaken the inquiring mind.

QUESTIONS FOR ANALYSIS OF PAPER *A*

This exercise answers its own questions so that you can understand what you are expected to do in analyzing the organization of the paragraphs.

1. What is the thesis statements of Paper *A*?

Answer: The thesis statement is the first sentence: *Lack of encouragement of creativity in the present school system discourages a real search for knowledge.*

2. How does the second paragraph support this thesis statement?

Answer: It gives and supports one reason for the validity of the thesis statement. It makes the point that the student is frequently graded on how well he follows form rather than on how deeply he thinks.

3. What is the function of the second sentence in the introductory paragraph?

Answer: This sentence does not belong in the introductory paragraph. It should be the first sentence of the second paragraph, because it is really the topic sentence of that paragraph. All the second paragraph is a discussion of the subject given in the second sentence of the introductory paragraph. Nowhere else in the paper is *following a certain form* discussed. The introductory paragraph should be revised so that it is a paragraph of about fifty to seventy-five words and not just a single sentence. The thesis statement should come at the end of the revised introductory paragraph.

4. How does the third paragraph support the thesis statement?

Answer: It gives and supports a second reason for the validity of the thesis statement. It makes the point that too frequently the student is rewarded for simply parroting the teacher's ideas and is penalized if he puts forward the result of his own thinking.

5. Which sentence is the topic sentence of the third paragraph?

Answer: The last sentence in the paragraph is the topic sentence. It would be better placed as the first sentence.

6. a. Which sentence is the topic sentence of the fourth paragraph?
   b. What is the function of this paragraph in the paper?

Answer: a. The first sentence in the fourth paragraph is the topic sentence.

   b. The fourth paragraph gives and supports a third reason for the validity of the thesis statement. It deplores the emphasis on insignificant details.

7. What is the function of the fifth paragraph?

Answer: The fifth paragraph sums up the points that have been made in support of the thesis statement. The paper would be more effectively organized if most of the material in the fifth paragraph were part of the revised introductory paragraph and if a concluding statement were placed at the end of the fourth paragraph. (This weakness in organization, especially demonstrated by the inadequacy of the introductory paragraph, is probably caused by the writer's failure to think through his subject before starting to write. He probably devised his support for the thesis statement as he wrote from paragraph to paragraph. Then when he got to the end he could see what his support was and summed it up there. It takes a skillful student to succeed at the organize-as-you-write plan. This student was not quite skillful enough.)

8. Does the sixth paragraph support the thesis statement? Does it belong in the paper? Why or why not?

Answer: The sixth paragraph does not support the thesis statement because it does not give and support a reason for the validity of the thesis. In fact, this paragraph does not belong in the paper because it introduces a second subject by attempting to explain what should be done about the situation. The subject of this paragraph could be explored and supported in another paper, not here.

9. Where should this paper end?

Answer: The paper should end with the fourth paragraph.

B.   EDUCATORS THAT DISCOURAGE THINKING

1. There is no doubt that today's public school student is lacking in creative thinking. He finds it far less trouble to develop a sort of mnemonic memorizing mind that follows but never leads. Therefore, most students prefer to memorize and leave tiresome thinking for later.

2. Classroom discussion is different. There students are often willing to shine forth orally, but never, never in writing. They would rather be asked to respond with a *T* for True and *F* for False on a simple and clear cut objective exam than be asked to think an issue through and discuss it in writing.

3. Students are inclined to drag their feet when it comes to showing their teacher, via clear and thorough essay-type discussions, that they have a full understanding of course content. But this is hardly the fault of the student, at least not in the high school that I attended. In fact, from the elementary level up to Grade 12, we were trained to memorize, and we soon learned that perfecting the practice of spouting out the outlined truths, with no time out for understanding and tying together of isolated facts, was the way to the best grades. We worked out the formula for success and we learned to like it, in the way any child learns to adapt to the security of a system.

4. If the nation is to continue to survive and even to progress, then such trends as this must be halted. Such lazy testing is developed for lazy grading, and the obvious answer is that teachers must begin to care enough to improve their methods. Teachers must be taught before they can teach; otherwise, the inquiring minds of our potential leaders will never be freed from the regimented, "fill-in-the-blank" type of nonthinking. It could even be that there is more truth in the ancient admonition: If you can't do it, teach it; if you can't teach it, teach others to teach it.

QUESTIONS FOR ANALYSIS OF PAPER B

1. The thesis statement of this paper is the last sentence of the first paragraph: *Most students prefer to . . . leave tiresome thinking for later.* The writer makes only one point in the remainder of the paper to support this thesis. What is it?

2. The second paragraph consists of only two sentences and does not give or support an idea. Could these two sentences be integrated into

any other paragraph in the paper? If so, which one? If not, why not?

3. The third paragraph is the only one that can be called a developmental paragraph. What topic sentence does it develop?

4. What is the purpose of the fourth paragraph? Does it contain material that might be used in the third paragraph? Is there another subject here that might be used as a topic sentence in support of the thesis statement? What is it?

5. Since the paper gives only one reason for the validity of the thesis statement, make up two more reasons that might be supported in developmental paragraphs. (The writer of this paper can handle the language fairly well. From all indications, however, he wrote this paper without much planning. The result is that the paper does not fully support its thesis, that some ideas and paragraphs are left undeveloped and that the whole ends with a vague *such trends as this must be halted*.)

C.   WHY STUDENTS NO LONGER INQUIRE

1. Today's high school students are not interested in "why." They prefer to be led to simple answers already set down for them, as they have always been led. They do not seek out solutions to problems of economics or geography or literature. In fact, one of the standard slogans at testing time at my high school was always: "We don't know the questions, just the answers." All we knew was what our teachers told us: just the facts. These we memorized, because memorizing is all that was ever required of us.

2. It seems to be a workbook world, and such a teaching method teaches nobody anything. In chemistry labs across the country, the student is handed tubes and burners and a problem to "solve." But he is shackled by the workbook at his elbow. Mix so-and-so much of *A* with this-and-that amounts of *B*. You get *C*. Here's what happened, and why. The student reacts with a yawn. The experiment got him nowhere. He discovered nothing, and he arrived at no conclusion but that one concluded for him.

3. When the same student is given something tangible to work toward, he shows his mettle. What did the word *slave* mean to Ancient Sparta? What was the real relationship between Philip and Alexander, and how do you know? Where's the proof of romanticism in Wordsworth's ode? How can that teacher call a triangle *beautiful*? Such questions stir a student to think and to research. He is challenged. He wants to know, and he will find out.

4. When a student is introduced to an unanswered problem, he cannot help working up an interest in finding an answer. He

wants to assume responsibility. Even if he arrives at only a half-right conclusion, at least he has had the freedom of investigating. He might, in his struggles, hit upon an original idea. How nice to have understood the question, to have cared enough to try for an answer, to have contributed to the world's knowledge.

QUESTIONS FOR ANALYSIS OF PAPER C

1. What is the thesis statement of Paper C?

2. What is the purpose of the rest of the introductory paragraph? Does this paragraph indicate any reasons for the validity of the thesis statement? If so, are these reasons developed and supported in the remainder of the paper?

3. The first sentence of the second paragraph is the topic sentence. What did the writer do in the remainder of the paragraph to establish his point as a valid one? Has he offered enough evidence to establish his point? What might be done to make the topic sentence valid?

4. Does the third paragraph support the topic sentence? Look at it closely. Does it give and support a second reason for the validity of the thesis statement? If so, is the evidence offered in support of the topic sentence enough to establish it as valid? If not, what is the purpose of the third paragraph?

5. In what way is the fourth paragraph related to the thesis statement? What is its purpose in the paper?

D.   THE CASE AGAINST FOOTBALL

1.   High school football is an outrageous waste. The game is too expensive: in dollars and cents, in hours and minutes, in morale, and in physical well-being. When gym equipment and coaching salaries grow more important than academic progress and class work waits upon athletics, when the student's sense of values is distorted and fine young bodies are deliberately exposed to physical violence, then football does indeed cost too much.

2.   Seldom does the total gate receipt for the season, even with the added dimes and quarters from concession stands, smooth out the balance. The school administrator and his staff pay top prices for dummies, pads, cleated shoes and face guards; their boys need and deserve the best possible protection out there on the field of danger. Turfs, sturdy bleachers, and weather-conditioned gymnasiums are theirs to maintain (with a giant slice of the school board's carefully balanced budget).

And the hiring of the go-gettingest coach available is one of the greatest expenses the school faces. But all that is the simple, red-and-black side of the ledger. Other problems growing out of football are far more important, though they may not be quite so obvious to the outsider.

3. The existing situation makes it almost shameful for a student to neglect his team in favor of class work. When there are posters to put out, tickets to sell, or athletic banquets to be arranged, the student is often expected to make the time, even during a class period, if the heat is on, to back the team. He can hardly be expected to pay more attention to his Biology III notebook than he pays to the Homecoming Game; why, it's practically a breach of faith! So he sets aside the biology assignment and the Latin translation, and the three chapters in the Hardy novel due tomorrow so he won't be late for the pep rally. After all, Miss Hopkins and those other teachers must realize (they've heard it all week over the intercom) that Coach Jamison and his boys need all the spirit that can be whipped up if they're to ring up another victory for Consolidated High. And therein lies another serious failure of the football centered school.

4. The song that resounds across the campus for the week is not an echo of that old softie that insists "It is not that we win or lose, but how we play the game!" None of that mush for the up-to-date pigskin elevens. It's no more who we play, but who we beat. The coach shouts out his determined promises, then the bugles blare for the captain Himself, the biggest imaginable Man on Campus. So long to the fellow with the *A* average and to all the other wearers of the letter sweater, the mark of the scholar. And often the school's reputation is built on its team's success, not on the number of serious students who go on to excel in their college studies. Still, all this is to say nothing of the deliberate exposure to physical dangers, even death, to which public schools subject their students in the glorious name of football. We'd rather not dwell on the number of boys who either don't make it at all or who are carried out between quarters to a life of lameness, of back or brain. Besides those caught in the crossfire on the gridiron, too, are those who suffer (or die) in automobile or school bus collisions en route to the Big Game.

5. There's no winner in high school football. When the count is taken of money, time, energy, and suffering spent on "the game," both teams have lost, no matter how many times the

boys first downed, touched down, touched back, or kicked goal. The real score (obscured by the glaring numbers on the great electric scoreboard) reads NOTHING to NOTHING.

(Note that this paper has five paragraphs instead of the four prescribed in the diagram of the five-hundred-word paper. The writer developed his fourth paragraph so fully that he felt the need for a concluding paragraph. The paper is stronger for it.)

1. Outline Paper *D* so that it fits the diagram for a five-hundred-word paper. Arrange the outline in this way:

Thesis Statement: ....

    Topic Sentence 1: ....

    Topic Sentence 2: ....

    Topic Sentence 3: ....

Concluding Statement: ....

2. Is Paper *D* well organized? Why or why not?

II. So that your instructor may discover how well you can manage a five-hundred-word paper now, try your hand at writing one to fit the pattern prescribed in this chapter. Start with this statement: "............................. University (College) suits me best," and develop at least three reasons for your choice of the school you attend.

2 Getting Started

The hardest part of composition, the student sometimes thinks, is getting the first words on paper. The difficulty arises because the beginning writer has not given enough thought, before he starts to write, to exactly what he needs to say. He has probably jotted down the assignment with the due date, then promptly forgotten all about it until that famous *last minute*. To avoid penalty for a late paper, he then fumbles around making false starts and never seeming to get the right idea across. He has failed to realize that *writing requires thought*, not only during the writing process but long before pen is put to paper. How much thought is needed depends upon the difficulty of the subject assigned, the student's knowledge of the subject, and his experience with it.

Even polished writers frequently think for days or weeks about what they are going to write before the right idea comes to them. Usually you will not have that much time, but you might be surprised at how much time you can find to think about a topic if you will take the opportunity while doing small chores that do not require your full attention. You have more than enough time to think, for instance, when you are breakfasting or bathing or shoveling snow or walking between classes or waiting for the elevator.

What you must think about when you find these spare moments are (1) the specific, limited subject you are going to write about, (2) the precise main point (or thesis) you are going to establish, and (3) the exact purpose of your paper.

Choosing a Subject

At the beginning of a writing course, your instructor will no doubt assign a definite topic for each paper and clearly define each paper's purpose. But sometimes you will simply be handed a broad subject or be sent to find your own. This could mean trouble unless you have learned to select and limit a topic so that it can be adequately treated in five hundred words.

You already know enough to write about—you have been places, seen things. You have had experiences, some of which are unique to you. These you can write about and use as evidence to support your contentions. Even if you have never left home, you have used your five senses: You have observed people, places, and things, you have formed opinions and impressions. You have been in school for at least twelve years now and have gathered knowledge and ideas. You have read billboards, newspapers, and books. Above all, you have formed some definite and strongly held opinions that you will be able to support in writing. Of course, you may find, as many students have, that you hold some opinions and ideas you cannot justify logically when you try to set them down on paper. But you do have a vast supply of material; all you have to do is recall it from your memory.

Suppose that you have selected four possible topics for your paper.

1. The Life of Abraham Lincoln
2. Dates I Have Had
3. My College
4. The Battles of the Civil War

Any of these topics could be used for a paper, depending on the length of the paper you are to write. For the first and fourth topics you would use material you had learned in school or from your reading plus possibly some extra reading and study for either. The second and third topics would come from your own experience and observation.

But none of them is suitable for development in a five-hundred-word paper. Volumes have already been written about the life of Abraham Lincoln; therefore, you could not write five hundred significant words about the whole life of Lincoln. Similarly, the second topic, as it stands, cannot be used as the subject of a five-hundred-word paper. No doubt you have dated several times by now, but you can say nothing meaningful about *all* your dates in a short paper. About all you can do is list them with a brief comment about each, and this will not get you far in an English composition course. It is best to select one date, or a part of one date, and say something significant about it. The third topic is the same. Any college has a number of parts—faculty, students, dormitories, courses, sports, student union, and so on—but you cannot possibly write about all these parts if you are going to include all them under a broad topic. If you select a topic such as the third, you are obligated to do so. Obviously, the last topic is unsatisfactory, too. No one can say anything meaningful about all the battles of the Civil War in five hundred words. You will need to think further before you start to write.

Limiting Your Subject

If you are to explain an idea, object, or process, you must confine your explanation to a single subject. You must examine one idea or establish one point. Limiting yourself to a single subject is called giving your paper direction, or unity. You cannot support a broad point in a paper of five hundred words. Single direction is easier when the subject is limited.

Suppose, for example, your instructor asks you to write a paper about your high school. This is a broad topic, for there are numerous possibilities for limited subjects—the teachers, the courses, the school's academic standing, the amount of homework assigned, the physical plant, the PTA, the students' social life, the governing body, athletics, or any number of other subjects. You cannot even touch upon all these subjects in a paper of five hundred words. Pick *one* of these subjects to write about, if you are to cover your point adequately. If you do not limit your subject in this way, your paper will lack single direction, and you will be supporting no point at all.

How do you go about limiting a subject? First, you must reject the notion that you have nothing to write about. You *do* have material for writing good papers. You have accumulated some knowledge in your lifetime (or else what have you been doing in school all this time?). You have had a variety of experiences; you have made observations of all sorts; and you have formed opinions.

Think about this list of broad topics.

Advertising	Dating	Movies	School
Ambitions	Education	Music	Sports
Boys	Family	Neighborhood	Television
Cars	Friends	People	Travel
Clothes	Girls	Prejudices	
College	Hobbies	Reading	
Community	Jobs	Recreation	

You could write a paper of five hundred words on any of these topics. In fact, if you put your mind to it, you can think of more general topics to write about. None of these, for instance, would allow you to use much of the knowledge you have gained in your study of literature or of history or of science. You have ample material to write about, and you need never be caught short in getting started on a paper, if you will put your mind to work, use your imagination, and think.

Once you have selected a general topic, or it has been assigned you, the job is barely begun. Although you *can* write a short paper on a broad topic, the odds are overwhelming that it will be a poor one, because you have not planned carefully enough. You have not limited the subject to one that can be covered in a relatively few words.

Limiting a subject is the process of dividing a general topic into its parts, selecting one of these parts, and then further limiting it. Suppose that from the list of general topics above you decided to write on *sports*. You must then begin to jot down possible divisions of this topic.

> College sports
> Amateur sports
> Professional sports
> High school sports

The next step is to select the one division you know enough about, or can find enough information on, to be certain of your ground. From that division list smaller subjects you might be able to cover in five hundred words. Suppose, since you would likely know more about high school sports than the others, you select that topic. But "High School Sports" is still too general, for you would have to give an account of all the sports of your school—football, basketball, golf, tennis, volley ball, baseball, swimming, and track. So limit the topic more severely; choose *football* as the specific subject you want to work with. Now, rack your brain for subjects about high school football and write them down. You might come up with a list like the one below.

FOOTBALL AS A HIGH SCHOOL SPORT

1. The Value of Football to My High School
2. The Value of High School Football to the Player

3. The Value of High School Football to the Nonplaying Student
4. The Effect of High School Football on My Community
5. Expense of High School Football
6. An Adequate Football Stadium for My High School
7. The Emphasis on Football in My High School
8. Safety Equipment for the High School Football Player
9. The Treatment of Football Players by the Teachers
10. The Academic Grades of Football Players
11. The Treatment of Football Players by Other Students
12. Student Support of Football
13. The Football Hero
14. The Experience of Playing on a High School Football Team

First, delete those topics that least appeal to you; then select the one you best understand, and you are under way. You are not ready to start writing yet, however, until you do more planning and thinking.

Framing Your Thesis Statement

A good thesis statement is vital to your paper. It is the main point you are going to make and support in your paper. This statement will shape your paper's direction more than anything else you do. Without it the paper can have no structure; with it the paper has a foundation for development. It gives you the main point and it gives you a purpose—to establish this point in the remainder of the paper. Where you put the thesis statement is important. You already know that the recommended position is at the end of the introductory paragraph. If you put it there, and if it is a good statement, you will be headed in the right direction for the remainder of the paper.

Writing a thesis statement is no different from writing any other sentence, except for the care you must take in framing the thesis as the main point of your paper. It has, as do other sentences, a subject area and a predicate area. The subject area of the thesis statement, as in all sentences, announces what is being written about (the subject of the sentence). The predicate area, as in all sentences, says something about the subject. A thesis statement is diagrammed on the next page.

Complete Thesis Statement

| SUBJECT + MODIFIERS | + | VERB + COMPLETERS + MODIFIERS |

Subject Area   Predicate Area

You have just studied the process of limiting a subject so that it can be handled in five hundred words, and you have read through a list of fourteen specific subjects derived from the broader topic "High School Football." Any one of these fourteen will serve in the subject area of a thesis statement. For instance, take the first one listed, "The Value of Football to My High School." This phrase could easily become the subject area of a thesis statement if you simply add a predicate area to it, but you would probably not want to use this exact phrase. Decide, instead, what you think the value of football is to your high school. You might decide that it has no value at all when the matter is closely examined. In fact, you might believe that it would be better if there were no football at your high school. In this case, you might frame a thesis statement such as this one (We will call your school Consolidated High):

Varsity football should be discontinued at Consolidated High.

Varsity football constitutes the subject area of this thesis statement, and *should be discontinued at Consolidated High* makes up the predicate area. For another example, suppose you want to write about the fifth subject on the list, "Expense of High School Football." You might decide that football is too expensive for what it gives the school. You might then frame this thesis statement:

Varsity football at Consolidated High is an outrageous waste.

Here *Varsity football at Consolidated High* is the subject area of the statement, and *is an outrageous waste* is the predicate area.

What this discussion emphasizes is that to frame a thesis statement you must do two things: (1) select a single, limited subject (subject area), and (2) say something about the subject (predicate area). There is a little more to it than this, however, as you might suspect. Look, then, a little closer at each of these directions for writing a thesis statement.

1. Select a Single, Limited Subject

If your paper is to have a single direction, it must develop a single subject. If your thesis statement contains more than one subject, it is not a good one because you are obligated to develop each subject. Consider this statement:

> Our student election is not being run properly and we must do something about it.

Here are two thesis statements. The first condemns existing procedures, and the second urges action to revise the faulty procedures; it is not clear to the reader which of these is the real point of the paper. This sentence is composed of two sentences (actually independent clauses) joined by the conjunction *and*. The two parts of this sentence have equal importance because they both have exactly the same construction. But both parts can be included in an acceptable thesis statement, if one part is changed to become less important than the other. Thus, the thesis statement can become this:

> Since our student election is not being run properly, we must do something about it.

Now, with the addition of the subordinating conjunction *since*, the first part of the sentence has been cast in a dependent clause, and it becomes subordinate to the second part of the sentence, which now contains the single subject and predicate areas for the thesis statement. However, this thesis statement would be much better if the dependent clause *Since our student election is not being run properly* were reduced even further to a phrase:

> We must correct improper procedures in our student election.

or

> Improper procedures in our student election must be corrected.

Each of these last two thesis statements has one specific subject area and one specific predicate area. For either, the remainder of a five-hundred-word paper would answer the question, *Why must we correct election procedures?*

2. Say Something About the Subject

What you say about the subject in the predicate area is the most important part of the thesis statement, for it is here that you give expression to your own point of view that is going to be explored and supported in the rest of the paper. This point of view will be the key to the content of your paper. Consequently, you must take considerable care to be certain that your point of view can be supported and that it is clear to the reader. To make it so, learn the following guidelines for the predicate area of the thesis statement.

a. *The predicate area must also be limited.* Even though you have gone through the process of limiting the subject of the thesis statement, you may find that when you write your statement it is still too broad to deal with. It probably demands limiting in the predicate area. Consider this thesis statement:

> The United States is the best of all countries.

Proving this thesis would be easy if you were planning to write several volumes, but you cannot do it in a short paper. The predicate area of this thesis, *is the best of all countries*, obligates the writer to prove that the United States is better than *any* other country. To fulfill this obligation, he would have to consider the economic, moral, religious, political, and social conditions in every country of the world and then contrast them to those in the United States. This is not possible in five hundred words. Similarly, a statement such as

> Lee was a greater general than Grant.

cannot be established without considering the campaigns of each general and then comparing them. Neither is this a job for a short paper.

b. *The predicate area of the thesis statement should present an argumentative point of view toward the subject.* If you are to establish a main point, or prove a thesis, your paper must be partially argumentative. After all, you are trying to explain to the reader that your point is a sound one. Your paper will have no other purpose than to establish the validity of this main point. You must argue your point by presenting all the logical reasons and sound evidence you can muster. Your thesis must be the trumpet's call that sounds the challenge—you on one side, your reader on the other. So be bold about it; issue your challenge clearly and forcefully, as if you were engaging in debate. Use no weak phrases such as "to me" or "in my opinion" in your thesis, nor anywhere else in your paper, for they leave with your reader the impression that you are merely stating an opinion and that you are apologetic about attempting to prove it. Step from the crowd and write something like these thesis statements:

> The high school student needs to write more.
>
> Lady Macbeth is more masculine than feminine.
>
> Watching television does not turn children to delinquency.
>
> Freshman English is a farce.
>
> Charles Dickens found American life bewildering.

Only by giving the thesis in a firm statement can you interest the reader in reading your paper. Even if the instructor is your only reader, his opinion of your paper will be better simply because you caught his attention.

Do not delude yourself, however, into thinking that a striking thesis statement alone will win you a good grade; the thesis still has to be properly developed and logically supported. Select a thesis you can believe in and support. If you do not believe what you say, neither will your reader, and *you are writing to convince your reader.*

c. *The predicate area must say something meaningful.* A thesis statement about which there can be no controversy, about which everyone agrees, can hardly result in a paper that anyone will want to read. If, for instance, you try to write a paper using a thesis like

> Travel by plane saves time.

or

> Good conservation practices help the farmer.

you are not going to get much of a reaction from your reader except "Ho-hum. So what?" And justifiably, for these statements are trite and meaningless.

d. *The predicate area must say something exact about the subject.* Look at this thesis statement:

Football is an exciting game.

The predicate area is made up of the phrase *is an exciting game.* If you were to write a paper on this thesis, its content must be controlled by the key word *exciting,* because it gives your paper its single direction. There is no other emotion or feeling you can write about in your paper. What exactly does *exciting* mean? It is hard to define. What might be exciting to one person might leave another cold. And there is the problem with such a predicate area—it does not get to a precise point. It is not exact. It allows the writer to say almost anything as long as it is in any way associated with football. Consequently, the writer can ramble and come to no specific point in his paper. To improve this statement, make an exact point about one variety of football:

Even touch football is dangerous.

You can see that the same difficulty exists in this thesis statement:

Macbeth makes fascinating reading.

If you are assigned a paper on *Macbeth,* make an exact point about the play:

Costuming Act I, scene vi, of *Macbeth* presents special difficulty.

A diagram of the process of framing a thesis statement will review what has been presented so far.

In this diagram, the broad topic might be one already suggested, "My School." For illustration, assume that your school is Glory University. To restrict this broad topic to a more manageable subject, you must then list the parts of that broad topic that you will be able to write about from your observation and experience. Would you choose sports, professors, dormitory life, registration

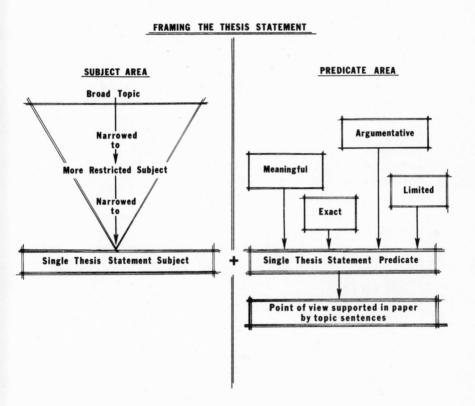

FRAMING THE THESIS STATEMENT

SUBJECT AREA   PREDICATE AREA

Broad Topic

Narrowed to

More Restricted Subject

Narrowed to

Argumentative

Meaningful

Exact

Limited

Single Thesis Statement Subject   +   Single Thesis Statement Predicate

Point of view supported in paper by topic sentences

day, academic work, or the student union? Because you have been through it recently, you might pick *registration day*. You now have a subject for the specific thesis statement of your five-hundred-word paper. To complete the statement, you must form the predicate area by saying something about the subject. What you say, of course, will depend on your own experience. You might say that you found registration day frustrating or tiring or confusing or inefficient or pleasant or efficient or none of these. For illustration, say that you found it confusing. You now have a thesis statement in its barest form:

Registration day was confusing.

In reaching a specific thesis statement you have gone through the process of selection shown by this diagram.

subject area

Topic

Subject Choices

predicate area

Point of View Choices

SPORTS — Frustrating

DORM LIFE — Confusing

PROFS — Inefficient

GLORY U.

Registration Day — Pleasant

ACADEMICS — Tiring

STUDENT UNION — Efficient

The large block on the left indicates the broad topic, "Glory University." The smaller blocks in the middle of the page represent six of the many restricted subjects that are a part of the broad topic. The shading of the fourth block shows that only one part, *registration day*, has been selected as the subject of the paper. The blocks on the right of the page show some of the many points of view that might have been formed about the subject, registration day. The shading of the block labeled *confusing* indicates the selection of a point of view toward the subject. Now, the content of the paper is restricted to the subject matter represented by the two shaded blocks. Material from no other block can be used in writing the paper. The paper may be concerned only with demonstrating that registration day was confusing. The key word that controls the content of the paper is *confusing*. Any material that does not establish the validity of that key word does not belong in the paper.

Now you have a thesis statement: *Registration day was confusing*. This statement, however, is not a particularly good expression of the thesis. First, because the paper is to concern Glory University as its broad topic, mention it in your thesis statement:

> Registration day at Glory University was confusing.

Everything being equal, a complex sentence, one that contains a dependent clause, will probably be best as a thesis statement, depending on the context of the introductory paragraph. So try a complex sentence:

> Although I had memorized every step I was to take, registration day at Glory University was confusing.

This sentence can be improved by making the verb active. Revise it to this version:

> Although I had memorized every step I was to take, registration day at Glory University confused me.

EXERCISES

A. Here are some thesis statements. Below each is a criticism based on the characteristics of a good thesis statement.

 1. Water skiing is more fun than any other sport I have tried.
    (The word *fun* in the predicate area is not exact. It is so 'vague

that anything associated with water skiing could be brought into the paper. What might be fun to one person might not be fun at all to another. In addition, the predicate is not sufficiently limited. Many sports would have to be compared to water skiing. A better thesis is *The water-skier has to be foolhardy*.)

2. Intercollegiate sports benefit the university and they build spirit in the student body.

(This thesis statement has two subjects, each of them in a separate independent clause. One or the other of these must be chosen as the thesis. The first clause about benefit to the university is too unlimited in the predicate area to be treated in five hundred words. One benefit might be appropriate: *The chief function of intercollegiate football is to advertise the university*. Both subjects can be included in the thesis statement, depending on the context in which the statement appears, if one is made into a less important dependent clause: *Although intercollegiate football builds spirit in the student body, its chief function is to advertise the university*. Now, the thesis statement is the independent clause of the sentence.)

3. College sports offer many advantages to the student.

(Neither the subject area nor the predicate area of this thesis statement is sufficiently limited. *College sports* can be divided into at least two parts—intramural and intercollegiate. As the thesis stands, which of these two parts would the paper discuss? *Many advantages* in the predicate is likewise too broad for five hundred words; so one advantage is enough to explore in the paper. A more limited thesis on this subject is: *Collegiate intramural sports shape the character of participating students*.)

B. Considering the characteristics of a good thesis statement, write a criticism of each of the following thesis statements. Some of these may be acceptable for development in five hundred words.
   1. The president's speech was very interesting and inspiring.
   2. Basketball fascinates me.
   3. Social fraternities encourage scholarship.
   4. My vacation in Europe was the most educational trip I have taken.
   5. Women drive as well as men do.
   6. People should consider all aspects of medicare.

Stating Your Purpose

Once you have written a good thesis statement, the next step is to add a *because* to it, and then jot down all the reasons you can think of for your point of view toward your subject. Suppose, for instance, you decided to use this thesis statement:

Interschool football should be discontinued at Consolidated High.

If you actually believe this statement, you should have little difficulty in listing a number of reasons for your belief. Your list might be something like the following:

Interschool football should be discontinued at Consolidated High because:
1. The school loses money on interschool football.
2. The average student is unable to participate in the game.
3. Players are seriously injured each year.
4. Students lose class time in activities supporting the team.
5. Students' attention is taken away from academic subjects.
6. Students lose study time attending pep rallies.
7. Trips to neighboring cities are dangerous.
8. The importance of the football player is overrated.
9. Football is likely to teach players the wrong set of values.
10. Too much attention is given to football at the expense of scholarship.
11. The coach seems more important than other teachers.
12. The cost of building and maintaining the stadium is high.
13. The value of the school is likely to be judged by the success of its football team.
14. The winning coach is paid a premium salary.
15. Winning at all costs becomes too important.

If you inspect this list, you can see that certain reasons may be grouped together because they are closely related. Some specific reasons may have to be left out and others may have to be modified so that you can get the grouping you want. The following is one way to arrange these reasons:

I. The cost of interschool football is prohibitive.
    A. The school loses money on interschool football.
    B. The cost of building and maintaining a stadium is high.
    C. The winning coach is paid a premium salary.

II. Scholarship is forced to take second place to football.
    A. Students lose class time in activities that support the team.
    B. Students' attention is taken away from academic study.
    C. Students lose study time attending pep rallies.
    D. Coaches seem more important than other teachers.

III. The effect of interschool football on the student body is deleterious.
    A. It builds the wrong set of values.

       1. Winning at any cost becomes too important.
       2. The importance of the star football player is magnified out of proportion.
       3. The school is judged by the success of its football team.
    B. Students are placed in unnecessary danger.
       1. Players are seriously injured each year.
       2. Students driving to out-of-town games invite tragedy.

You now have ample material to write your paper—so much, in fact, you may not want to use it all. But you can use it all by writing it up in three developmental paragraphs preceded by a brief introductory statement.

Now that the material to be used has been arranged in a logical order (but by no means the only one), you are ready to write a purpose statement. In the purpose statement, you tell exactly what your paper will cover and how you are going about it. It will not become a part of your paper, but it is important to you in giving direction and organization to your paper. Your instructor may ask you to turn in a purpose statement for each paper you write. A purpose statement for a paper using the material arranged from the thesis on football might turn out like this:

> In this paper, I intend to support the main point that interschool football should be discontinued at Consolidated High because (1) the cost of interschool football is prohibitive, (2) scholarship is forced to take second place to football, and (3) the effect of interschool football on the student body is deleterious.

With the writing of this purpose statement, you have most of your paper done. This type of planning makes the actual writing much easier, and the work will go smoothly if you know how to present logical support in well-ordered paragraphs.

Look again at the introductory paragraph of the paper about college fraternities.

> At many colleges and universities—particularly among those in the South—the social fraternity, not the classroom, is the chief concern of the student body. *These social fraternities are undesirable in American universities* because they are expensive, they are detrimental to academic achievement, and they lack democracy.

You already know that the thesis statement here is that social fraternities are undesirable in American universities. Notice, however, that this independent clause is followed by three "because" clauses, giving the reader and writer a guide to the organization of the paper. With these three dependent clauses the reader has a quick summary of the paper, listing only its main points in support of the thesis statement. He expects the writer to develop the first clause in the first section of the paper after the introductory paragraph, the second clause in the second section, and the third clause in the third section. In the five-hundred-word paper, a section is a paragraph. In a longer paper, a section might consist of several paragraphs.

EXERCISES

A. Here are some broad topics. Select three of these, and for each make a list of the parts into which each can be divided. Each list should contain at least six or seven parts.

Advertising	Education	People
Ambitions	Family	Prejudices
College	Marriage	Reading
Community	Movies	Television
Dating	Music	Travel

B. From the list you composed in Exercise A, select five parts (with at least one part from each list) and write a good thesis statement for each of the five subjects.

C. You may not have agreed with the paper about football in the last chapter, so copy the following diagram and fill it in, taking the opposite view. Start with a thesis statement that says something like *Football is the best thing that ever happened to our high school,* and give your reasons. Make your reasons and your support for the reasons as strong as you possibly can. Do not forget to put your most persuasive reason last.

Thesis Statement: ....
   (The thesis statement is valid because. . . .)

   Reason 1: ....
      (Reason 1 is valid because. . . .)

      Reason A: ....
      Reason B: ....
      Reason C: ....
         (The thesis statement is valid because. . . .)

Reason 2: ....

     (Reason 2 is valid because. . . .)

Reason A: ....

Reason B: ....

Reason C: ....

     (The thesis statement is valid because. . . .)

Reason 3: ....

     (Reason 3 is valid because. . . .)

Reason A: ....

Reason B: ....

Reason C: ....

Concluding Statement: ....

D. Write a purpose statement from the outline you composed in Exercise C.

E. Write a five-hundred-word paper from the outline for Exercise C.

Maintaining Unity
and Coherence

3 Each five-hundred-word paper works toward clarifying a single point, and every statement in the paper pushes toward a single objective: convincing the reader that the thesis statement is valid. Thus, the paper needs unity—singleness of tone and purpose. And, although every paragraph and every sentence furthers that sole intent, each of the paper's parts must hold together to keep the reader's attention. Coherence devices hold paragraph to paragraph and sentence to sentence to allow the reader safe and undisturbed passage from thought to thought in support of the thesis statement. Unity is the "togetherness" of the whole paper, whereas coherence is the means we use to insure that the individual parts flow naturally and easily from one to another.

UNITY

Unity means oneness. In all the writing you do, whether it is a sentence or a book, you will have to be concerned with this oneness. Perhaps the simplest way to explain unity is by an analogy with a compass. The compass gives direction. You can, by following a specific compass direction, move steadily south or east or north or west or in any direction between these main points. But if you do not follow one point on the compass, you will never reach a goal. Say, for instance, you wanted to arrive at a spot east of your position. You go toward that spot as long as you follow east on your compass, but if you veer south and then west, you obviously will never arrive. The same is true of writing. Start in a single direction and stick to it, never veering. Unity in writing is a matter of direction, that is, of maintaining the *single* direction you began with.

When you write a paper, the thesis statement gives you a single direction to be followed throughout the paper. The paper must consist of support for the single point of your thesis statement. In the paragraph, the topic sentence gives you that single direction. If you deviate from directly supporting either a thesis statement or a topic sentence, you violate the principle of unity. This is why it is so important to use care in framing the thesis statement and the topic sentences of your papers.

Look, for instance, at the following paragraph.

> European castles still standing prove that life in those great damp structures was far from comfortable. Cold, wet drafts blew through the long corridors, and heating such a barn was difficult and expensive. Although many bedrooms had fireplaces in them, the beds still had to be heavily curtained in winter before the occupants could keep from freezing to death. Walls were draped with tapestries and curtains to keep the cold winds out of other rooms. Five hundred years ago, it might have been easy for a lord to retain a hundred carpenters to build enough heavy oak pieces to furnish his manor, but today such an undertaking would cost thousands of dollars. For instance, just installing wall-to-wall carpeting in one of the gigantic rooms would make a dent in a multimillionaire's bank roll. And think of the staff that would have to be maintained if a castle were to be lived in today. There would be the kitchen help, a whole battalion of housekeepers, several moat cleaners, and an army of grounds keepers.

This paragraph may, at first reading, seem to be fairly good; but look at it again, and you will see that it does not move in a single direction even if it is concerned only with castles. The paragraph actually moves in three different directions. First, it tells how uncomfortable castles were and how their inhabitants met this discomfort. Second, it mentions how much money it would cost to furnish such castles today, and finally, it veers to the subject of domestic help. So, the paragraph contains three subjects and moves in three directions. Consequently, it reaches no goal because none of the three subjects is adequately developed, and certainly the principle of unity is violated. A unified paragraph could be written on any one of these subjects.

The following paragraph, although written tongue-in-cheek, discusses the cost of castlekeeping:

> At today's prices, maintaining a castle in the way the feudal lords of the middle ages did would be impossible even for the Really Rich. Any castle worth mentioning needed a big enough staff of domestics to at least keep the chewed-on bones shoveled up off the mead hall floor while the fulltime silversmith hammered out the amulets for next week's dragon slayers. Then there would have to

be thatch put on the gardener's hut while he replanted the rosemary and thyme, and scullery jacks and jills to turn the pig on the spit in the galley. Menservants stood by in platoons to weld the knights into their armor and to let down the drawbridge and grind it up again if the Danes tried sneaking through. Add knights and embroidered squires waiting permission to Crusade, and pink and pretty ladies-in-waiting standing by to deliver the next sonnet to Milady's courtly lover. Add the cost for all this to the expense of feeding the Poor Porters, the cellarful of emaciated unknowns, and the fishes in the moat. The monthly expense of the noble family's entourage would be enough to eat the heart out of any modern multimillionaire's paycheck.

This paragraph develops only one subject—a multimillionaire today could not afford the upkeep of a medieval castle—and it sticks to that subject from start to finish. This is what you must do to maintain unity in your writing.

Here is another paragraph for analysis. Read through it to see if you think it maintains unity.

Egypt was civilized long before there was any written history of the country. Egypt has an area of 386,000 square miles. Ancient Egyptians knew so much about embalming that some of their mummies are preserved for us to view in museums. The people of the world are concerned about saving these treasures, and others, now that the course of the Nile River is to be altered in the next decade. The Egyptians carried on commerce with neighboring nations. They studied and were successful with military strategy. For a time they lived under a system of government-controlled production. There is a wide area of fertile farmland along the Nile River. The early Egyptians built great halls and temples whose ruins still stand. Without modern machinery, they built the great pyramids near Cairo. Tourists come in great numbers each year to visit them. Today Cairo is the country's hurried and noisy commercial capital. Long before the birth of Christ, Egyptians knew how to turn wastelands into arable fields. They encouraged the arts and held great meetings where learned men gathered. They were always a religious people, holding to their beliefs in many gods until about 1400 B.C. when Aton, the single god who represented the life-giving power of the sun, was established as the Egyptian deity. In 1945, Egypt gained charter membership in the United Nations.

You see quickly that this paragraph does not maintain unity but that it races from subject to subject, each loosely associated with Egypt. To analyze this paragraph, look first at the opening sentence.

According to the organizational diagram for the five-hundred-word paper in the last chapter, this sentence is the topic sentence for the paragraph. That is, it specifically announces the subject the paragraph is going to be concerned with. This sentence gives the paragraph its single direction.

The opening sentence of the paragraph is: *Egypt was civilized long before there was any written history of the country*. If the remainder of the paragraph is to support this topic sentence and to be concerned with no other subject, the sentence must contain a word or phrase that can be called the pointer. It points to the single direction the remainder of the paragraph must follow to be unified. The topic sentence about Egypt has such a pointer. The word *civilized* controls the direction the paragraph will follow. If any sentence does not prove that Egypt was civilized, it does not belong in the paragraph, and it must be deleted.

For purposes of analysis, here are the sentences of the paragraph listed and numbered.

1. Egypt has an area of 386,000 square miles.
2. Ancient Egyptians knew so much about embalming that some of their mummies are preserved for us to view in museums.
3. It is these treasures that the world is concerned about saving.
4. Early Egyptians carried on commerce with neighboring nations.
5. They studied and were successful with military strategy.
6. They lived under a system of government-controlled production.
7. A wide area of fertile farmland edges the Nile.
8. The Egyptians built great halls and temples whose ruins still stand.
9. Without modern machinery, they built the great pyramids near Cairo.
10. Tourists come in great numbers each year to view Egypt's ruins.
11. Long before the birth of Christ, Egyptians knew how to turn wastelands into arable fields.
12. They encouraged the arts and held great meetings where learned men gathered.
13. They were always a religious people.

14. In 1945, Egypt gained charter membership in the United
    Nations.

These sentences need to be analyzed one at a time to see if they
give support to the pointer word, *civilized*, in the topic sentence.
Sentence 1, since it tells about the land area of Egypt, has nothing
to do with Egypt's being civilized. It does not support the topic
sentence. Delete it. Sentence 2, which tells about the Egyptians'
knowledge of embalming, does support the idea that Egypt was
civilized, so it may remain a part of the paragraph. Sentence 3
says that the world is concerned about saving Egyptian treasures,
but because it discusses the present world's concern and not Egypt's
past, it must be eliminated if the paragraph is to follow a single
direction. Sentence 4, about Egypt's commerce with neighboring
nations, can be retained because it does explain Egypt's past civilization, as can 5 and 6, about the early Egyptians' knowledge of
military strategy and control of production. Sentence 7 must be left
out; the fact that there is fertile farmland in Egypt does not prove
that Egypt was civilized. But that the Egyptians built great halls,
temples, and pyramids—sentences 8 and 9—does prove their civilization, so they stay. The number of tourists who visit Egypt does not
prove that Egypt was civilized because tourists often visit places that
have never been civilized. So sentence 10 must go. Sentence 11,
which tells about the Egyptians' farming abilities, does indicate
that ancient Egyptians were civilized, and this sentence can be retained. Any nation that cultivates the arts and holds conferences of
learned men would be said to have a fairly high level of civilization.
Sentence 12, then, should stay in the paragraph. Sentence 13, about
the Egyptians' religious feelings, does not necessarily establish their
civilization; for uncivilized peoples also have deep religious in-
clinations, and the sentence must be deleted. That Egypt gained
charter membership in the United Nations has nothing to do with
Egypt's past civilization. It is concerned with the present only, and
so sentence 14 will have to be left out.

Eliminating those sentences not supporting the topic sentence
with its pointer leaves these:

1. ~~Egypt has an area of 386,000 square miles.~~
2. The ancient Egyptians knew so much about embalming
   that some of their mummies are preserved for us to view
   in museums.

3. ~~It is these treasures that the world is concerned about saving.~~
4. Early Egyptians carried on commerce with neighboring nations.
5. They studied, and were successful with, military strategy.
6. They lived under a system of government-controlled production.
7. ~~A wide area of fertile farmland edges the Nile.~~
8. The Egyptians built great halls and temples whose ruins still stand.
9. Without modern machinery they built the great pyramids near Cairo.
10. ~~Tourists come in great numbers each year to view Egypt's ruins.~~
11. Long before the birth of Christ, Egyptians knew how to turn wastelands into arable fields.
12. They encouraged the arts and held great meetings where learned men gathered.
13. ~~They were always a religious people.~~
14. ~~In 1945, Egypt gained charter membership in the United Nations.~~

The remaining sentences can be put together into a unified paragraph, but it is not a well-developed nor readable one.

Egypt was civilized long before there was any written history of the country. These ancient people knew so much about embalming that some of their mummies are preserved for us to view in museums. These people carried on commerce with neighboring nations. They studied, and were successful with, military strategy. They lived under a system of government-controlled production. The Egyptians built great halls and temples whose ruins still stand. Without modern machinery, they built the great pyramids near Cairo. Long before the birth of Christ, Egyptians knew how to turn wastelands into arable fields. They encouraged the arts and held great meetings where learned men gathered.

Now, with all the material that does not directly support the topic sentence deleted, the paragraph is at least unified. All the remaining sentences support the idea that ancient Egypt was civilized.

Here is one more paragraph for analysis of its unity.

The composition student, in one year alone, sees enough waste to permanently destroy his sense of well-being. He sacrifices fifty minutes a day, five days a week, thirty-six weeks of the otherwise useful year. If his scooter is missing or if Mary Lou wasn't home when he called last night or if breakfast was burned, it's hard for him to keep his mind on paper writing. No matter how full of vitality he is when he marches into the classroom, the essay writer droops away, physically exhausted, when the final bell rings. One of those "dedicated" teachers can turn a potential writer into a nervous, quaking mouse with her constant shoulder-tapping, head-shaking and advice-giving. Even the most enthusiastic student is ready to give up when he has to be listening always to reprimands about spelling and where to put the semicolon. Writing is bad enough, but writing under such a dictator who denies the classroom citizen his basic freedoms is unbearable. Writing materials are wasted, too. High school students have to buy ball point pens for one class, cartridge pens for another, and compasses and drawing pencils for others. It's sometimes pretty difficult to figure out how the Public Education System can call itself "free." Some of the less expensive notebooks fall apart when one semester is about half through, which means probably the notebook was not a wise choice after all.

The topic sentence of this paragraph is, as expected, the first sentence in the paragraph: *The composition student, in one year alone, sees enough waste to permanently destroy his sense of well-being.* The pointer here is the word *waste.* Any sentence that does not show the waste a composition student sees does not belong in this paragraph. This paragraph can also be analyzed by considering each sentence separately to determine if it is following the direction the pointer indicates. This time the sentences that do not follow this direction, that is, that do not support the idea of waste in composition, are marked through.

1. He sacrifices fifty minutes a day, five days a week, thirty-six weeks of the otherwise useful year.
2. ~~If his scooter is missing, or if Mary Lou wasn't at home when he called last night, or if breakfast was burned, it's hard for him to keep his mind on paper writing.~~
3. No matter how full of vitality he is when he marches into the classroom, the essay writer droops away, physically exhausted, when the final bell rings.
4. ~~One of these "dedicated" teachers can turn a potential writer into a nervous, quaking mouse with her constant shoulder-tapping, headshaking, and advice-giving.~~

5. ~~Even the most enthusiastic student is ready to give up when he has to be listening always to reprimands about spelling and where to put semicolons.~~
6. ~~Writing is bad enough, but writing under such a dictator who denies the classroom citizen his basic freedoms is~~ unbearable.
7. Writing materials are wasted, too.
8. ~~High school students have to buy ball point pens for one class, cartridge pens for another, and compasses and drawing pencils for others.~~
9. ~~It's sometimes pretty difficult to figure out how the Public Education System can call itself "free."~~

This analysis indicates that only three sentences out of the whole paragraph follow the direction indicated by the pointer.

1. He sacrifices fifty minutes a day, five days a week, thirty-six weeks of the otherwise useful year.
2. No matter how full of vitality he is when he marches into the classroom, the essay writer droops away, physically exhausted, when the final bell rings.
3. Writing materials are wasted, too.

Put in their simplest form, these three sentences say that the composition student who writes in class wastes his time, his vitality, and his materials.

At this point, you are no doubt concluding that a paragraph is simply a short paper, as indeed it is. The methods of development are the same for both. Both have a single, central thought that is to be explored and developed. For the paper, that central thought is contained in the thesis statement; in the paragraph, it is contained in the topic sentence. As in the thesis statement, the predicate area of the topic sentence contains the pointer word, or phrase, that is the key to the content of the paragraph and consequently, to the single direction of the paragraph.

Look again, for instance, at the paragraph about the composition student and waste. It leads off with a topic sentence: *The composition student, in one year alone, sees enough waste to permanently destroy his sense of well-being.* In its predicate area, the single word *waste* is the pointer. The rest of the paragraph answers the question, *Why does the student see waste?* It gives three reasons:

The student sees waste because (1) he wastes his time, (2) his vitality, and (3) his writing materials. The paragraph will be unified as long as it sticks to developing these three reasons.

A unified paragraph can be illustrated by a diagram.

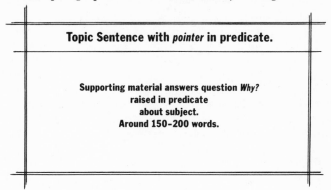

Topic Sentence with *pointer* in predicate.

**Supporting material answers question *Why?*
raised in predicate
about subject.
Around 150–200 words.**

EXERCISES

A. Pick out the pointer in each of the following topic sentences.

1. We are a frustrated generation.
2. Vague words can be useful.
3. History has indicated that these rulers were unduly optimistic.
4. Reasoning from analogy is dangerous.
5. The small car has suffered an astounding decline in popularity.
6. Reason is opposed to dogmatism.
7. Marriage demands cooperation between husband and wife.
8. Chaos reigned everywhere.
9. The good cook needs only a few simple rules.
10. The computer has changed management procedures.

B. For each of the following paragraphs, first write down the pointer in the topic sentence, and then list by number the sentences that support the pointer.

1.

(1) The family predicted that Jodie would some day make a fine veterinarian. (2) He had always shown a real tenderness toward animals. (3) Stray dogs and cats seemed to collect around the farm. (4) Once a beautiful, trained Collie showed up and never left again, but that wasn't as surprising as the pair of sleek Siamese cats that

moved in. (5) Those cats killed every rat in the barn inside of a week. (6) Animals all loved Jodie, too. (7) Folks used to drive out from town on Sundays to look at the whole families of painted buntings that ate with Jodie's chickens. (8) He kept Rhode Island Reds, mostly. (9) They say the bunting is rare in this part of the state. (10) Jodie was the quickest kid for learning things. (11) His teachers every one had nothing but praise for him. (12) He was never content to play until he had all of his homework done. (13) And he never missed a Sunday but once, going to church all through grammar school.

2.

(1) Elmer Dugan studied the coffee table. (2) There was something embarrassing about it, he realized. (3) The bowl of slightly melted Christmas candy should have been cleaned and refilled weeks ago. (4) Beside the candy jar sat an ashtray running over with bobby pins, bits of rick rack and three spools of yellow thread. (5) Next to the ashtray was the current issue of *Wild and Free* magazine, the trashy literature his wife and her good friend next door read and traded constantly. (6) John Thompson was getting a little nervous. (7) Elmer hoped that John and his loud-mouthed wife would get bored enough to leave soon. (8) But they didn't, and Elmer's gaze wandered to the second tier of the coffee table. (9) Adele Thompson was raving on about her eight-year old's ballet accomplishments. (10) She could go on forever, and Mary kept encouraging the chatter. (11) Elmer counted eight magazines on the second shelf of the coffee table, and one darning egg. (12) He supposed the darning egg had its rights, but why couldn't Mary keep it on the thirty-nine dollar, three-legged, Early American rock maple sewing stand she had insisted he buy for her last Christmas. (13) What he saw next, and couldn't believe, was a small, dead, and dried scorpion that Mary had reported killing three weeks ago. (14) The phone rang, a wrong number, and Adele Thompson started in on one of her favorite and most boring of all topics, the community and its telephone manners.

3.

(1) It was plain to the doctor that his day was going to be dreary. (2) Already twelve patients waited in the outer office. (3) The happy Tiller teenager giggled over a comic book as she rolled up her sleeve for her shot. (4) It was a joy to chat for a moment now and then with a happy, well, and well-adjusted kid. (5) It didn't improve the day, either, to be haunted by the difficult tonsilectomy facing

him Monday morning. (6) By mid-afternoon poor old Mrs. Clark would come begging for another bottle of sugar pills to pull her through another half-dozen "heart attacks." (7) The Everson infant needed surgery, but there was no convincing his backward parents, and the telephone jangled constantly. (8) Both the Mumford twins were down with a dangerous relapse. (9) Not that he had really hoped to fish tomorrow, but already a cold mist was falling. (10) By morning his little world would be iced over. (11) At least Nurse Hearne wouldn't be around to annoy him. (12) Never again. (13) He had let her go gladly when she demanded a sizeable pay raise and an extra half-day off. (14) He meditated for the length of one cigarette, coughed, and studied the frayed edge of his office carpet. (15) Craig Adams' test had come back positive, of course, and young Mrs. Adams would go into hysterics. (16) It would take until closing time to calm her. (17) And the town drunk, in for another Cure, was at this moment passing out in the waiting room.

C.   Read this paragraph by E. B. White.

It is a miracle that New York works at all. The whole thing is implausible. Every time the residents brush their teeth, millions of gallons of water must be drawn from the Catskills and the hills of Westchester. When a young man in Manhattan writes a letter to his girl in Brooklyn, the love message gets blown to her through a pneumatic tube—*pfft*—just like that. The subterranean system of telephone cables, power lines, steam pipes, gas mains and sewer pipes is reason enough to abandon the island to the gods and the weevils. Every time an incision is made in the pavement, the noisy surgeons expose ganglia that are tangled beyond belief. By rights New York should have destroyed itself long ago, from panic or fire or rioting or failure of some vital supply line in its circulatory system or from some deep labyrinthine short circuit. Long ago the city should have experienced an insoluble traffic snarl at some impossible bottleneck. It should have perished of hunger when food lines failed for a few days. It should have been wiped out by a plague starting in its slums or carried in by ships' rats. It should have been overwhelmed by the sea that licks at it on every side. The workers in its myriad cells should have succumbed to nerves, from the fearful pall of smoke-fog that drifts over every few days from Jersey, blotting out all light at noon, and leaving the high offices suspended, men groping and depressed, and the sense of world's end. It should have been touched in the head by the August heat and gone off its rocker.[1]

[1] E. B. White, *Here Is New York*, pp. 24–25. Copyright 1949 by E. B. White. Used by permission of Harper & Row, Publishers, Inc.

This paragraph maintains unity through its tight organization. To determine its organization, answer the following questions.

1. What is the topic sentence of the paragraph? What is the pointer?
2. Two principal reasons are given in support of the topic sentence and its pointer. What are they?
3. These two reasons also have supporting details to establish their validity. Write down the two principal reasons supporting the topic sentence, one at the head of one column and one at the head of another. Then, making two columns, list the supporting details for each of the two reasons.

COHERENCE

The concept of coherence is abstract, yet the writer must understand and get the feel of it before he can be sure he is communicating. We have already discussed unity, the logical relationship between sentences that allows them to move in a single direction. Coherence is unity's kinsman, but coherence differs from unity in that it is the mechanical connection that holds sentences or paragraphs together. When a writer uses certain writing techniques and devices in such a way as to guide the reader smoothly from one thought to another, his sentences stick together; they cohere.

Coherence does not necessarily follow as an inevitable result of achieving unity in writing. If unity is a matter of direction, then *coherence is a matter of connection.* This connection is ordinarily supplied by the writer, either consciously or unconsciously, in writing that is already unified. Coherence is not a part of unity and indeed, is not basically even a part of the thought of the paragraph or of the sentences being connected by a coherence device. Perhaps an analogy with a chain will help make coherence clear. A whole piece of chain is one with all the links interlocking. This interlock binds the whole together. Without it, there is no chain. Only separate links remain. So it is with writing. The interlock in writing is the coherence devices that bind sentences and paragraphs into a whole.

Consider, for instance, these two sentences taken out of context:

> Mr. and Mrs. Vitek thought that under the circumstances there was only one course to take. The young man on my left saw several alternatives.

These two sentences are on the same subject, but the second sentence appears at first glance to be on another subject because of the mention of an unnamed *young man*. The reader must pause to get his bearings when he reaches the second sentence because of this apparent change in subject. He is momentarily confused. Yet note that the addition of one word, *but*, before the first word in the second sentence avoids this confusion:

> Mr. and Mrs. Vitek thought that under the circumstances there was only one course to take. But the young man on my left saw several alternatives.

Now, the reader can go easily from the first sentence to the second with no pause, with no confusion. The two sentences are drawn together by the one word *but*. The use of such a transition word is one method of achieving coherence. There are more.

1. Coherence Through Consistent Point of View

Consider the following paragraph.

> A year spent teaching in the "shacks" adjacent to the city schools provides a unique education to any teacher. The classroom temperature gets awfully cold sometimes. You cannot imagine how hard it is to teach when it is forty-six degrees inside the building. Field mice race over the student lockers just as the teacher begins an important assignment. As summer approaches with its rising temperatures and increased noise level, the teacher has decided that she would gladly trade her unique experience for anyone's traditional classroom. The water fountain is so far away that it occupies a good part of the class time for teacher and students to get a drink.

This paragraph is unified. In the first sentence, *unique education* is the pointer, and the remainder of the paragraph shows how the teacher gets this education from teaching in the shacks. But it is not coherent. The reader is not led smoothly from sentence to sentence. The reason is obvious; the writer has not maintained a consistent point of view. *Point of view* is the position from which the writer looks at his subject. In this paragraph, the writer has shifted his position from sentence to sentence, and the reader has difficulty following his shifts. You can see the shift by picking out the subject of each sentence after the topic sentence. The subject of the second sentence is *temperature*. The subject of the third sentence is *you*. The fourth uses *field mice*; the fifth, *teacher*; and the sixth, *water fountain*. Therein lies the trouble with coherence in the paragraph. Because the paragraph obviously concerns a teacher and her experiences, each sentence should be about the teacher. A simple revision of this paragarph, using *teacher* as the subject of each sentence, greatly improves coherence.

> A year spent teaching in the "shacks" adjacent to the city schools provides a unique education to any teacher. *She* learns to adjust to a temperature of forty-six degrees inside her classroom, a condition that persists although all the radiators are working at full capacity. *She* learns to cope with the problem of field mice racing over the student lockers just as she begins an important assignment. As summer approaches with its rising temperatures and increased noise level, the *teacher* has decided she would gladly trade her unique experience for anyone's traditional classroom. *She* learns self control of thirst and teaches this lesson to her students, since the water fountain is so far away it is almost impossible to get a drink.

Now, the subject of all the sentences after the topic sentence is *teacher* (or its pronoun substitute, *she*), and as a result, the point of view is consistent. Note that in making the subject the same throughout, other improvements have been made almost automatically, and the whole paragraph is better.

2. *Coherence Through Chronological Order of Sentences*

Chronological order means simply the order in which events happen. This order is seen most often in narrative—writing that tells a story—and narrative is often a part of expository writing, particularly in illustrating a point. Narrative is not necessary, however, to the use of chronological order. For instance, a chronological order may be superimposed on the revised paragraph about the teacher, and the coherence of the paragraph becomes even stronger. Look at this revision.

> A year spent teaching in the "shacks" adjacent to the city schools provides a unique education to any teacher. *In the fall*, the teacher learns to cope with the problem of field mice racing over the student lockers just as she begins an important assignment. *In the winter*, she learns to adjust to a temperature of forty-six degrees, a condition that persists inside the classroom although all the radiators are working at full capacity. *In the spring*, she learns self control of thirst and teaches this lesson to her students, since a trip to the water fountain occupies a good part of the class time. *In summer*,

with its rising temperatures and increased noise level, she has decided that she would gladly trade the unique setting for anyone's traditional classroom.

This version, as indicated by the italicized phrases, takes the teacher through the seasons in chronological order during the school year, and overlaying the chronological order has resulted in beneficial changes. Note here that not just one method of gaining coherence is used alone in a paragraph but that methods are combined within any one paragraph.

3. Coherence Through Repetition of Key Words

Read through the following paragraph and notice the words that are connected by lines.

> This doctrine of the relativity of morals, though it has recently received an impetus from the studies of anthropologists, was thus really implicit in the whole scientific mentality. It is disastrous for morals because it destroys their entire traditional foundation. That is why philosophers who see the danger signal, from the time at least of Kant, have been trying to give to morals a new foundation, that is, a secular or nonreligious foundation. This attempt may very well be intellectually successful. Such a foundation, independent of the religious view of the world, might well be found. But the question is whether it can ever be a practical success, that is, whether apart from its logical validity and its influence with intellectuals, it can ever replace among the masses of men the lost religious foundation. On that question hangs perhaps the future of civilization.[2]

In this paragraph, the word *morals* appears in the first three sentences. *Foundations*, the key word repeated most often, appears five times. *Question* appears twice, and *trying* and *attempt* are synonymous enough to be repetitions. This repetition of key words would likely not be noticed on a first reading, if the words were not marked as they are here, and that is the way it should be. But this method of achieving coherence, when the paragraph is analyzed, appears to be the chief means of holding the paragraph together.

The author of the above paragraph is an experienced and successful writer; he uses this method of achieving coherence well. The beginning writer, however, must use caution to prevent the method

[2]W. T. Stace, "Man Against Darkness," *The Atlantic Monthly*. Copyright 1948 by *The Atlantic Monthly*. Reprinted by permission of *The Atlantic Monthly*.

itself from becoming obvious and obtrusive. In this example, a student has attempted to use repetition of key words to achieve coherence.

It is necessary for a student to receive a balanced education before he goes to college. This balanced education will help him decide what his goal is and how to achieve it. This balanced education will also help him if he fails in his endeavors by giving him the necessary background to start in another field of work. With this balanced education a student. . . .

In this example, the student has repeated *balanced education* four times in four sentences in an attempt at coherence. He has succeeded, however, only in annoying his reader by starting three of the four sentences with these same words. The student removed the annoying repetition and came up with this more successful version.

A student entering college needs a balanced high school education. It will help him decide what his goal in college is and how he will achieve that goal. It will enable him to choose from more than one college curriculum, if he finds his first choice unsatisfactory or if he fails in that field. With it a student. . . .

4. Coherence Through Spatial Order of Sentences

In using a spatial order to achieve coherence, a writer explains or describes objects as they are arranged in space. To describe a room a writer might, from a position in a doorway to the room, begin describing the wall to his right, go to the wall opposite him, to the wall on his left, and from there to the center of the room. In this way, the writer imposes an order on his material that helps to give it coherence. Examine this paragraph.

The main characteristic of the little farm we had walked over was disorder. The winding, narrow road was bumpy and rough, and weeds grew rank and tall on each side of it. Near the barn stood a battered, unpainted tractor, plow, and rake. On the other side of the road, weeds sapping life-giving substances from the soil were also growing among the small, withered cotton plants. The house needed paint and repairs. The steps and porch were rickety, and several of their boards were broken. The fence around the pasture was badly in need of repairs. The broken window panes in the house had pieces of tin and boards over them. On one side of the road lay bundles of grain decaying from long exposure to wind, rain, and sunshine. The wire was broken in many places, and the wooden posts, rotten at the ground, were supported by the rusty wire. The yard was littered with rubbish—tin cans, broken bottles, and paper.

The barn lacked paint; its roof sagged and some shingles needed to be replaced. In the pasture, diseased with weeds and underbrush, grazed thin, bony cattle, revealing their need for more and better food and shelter.

This paragraph has unity. The pointer in the topic sentence is *disorder*. All the details in the paragraph indicate the disorder on the little farm. But it lacks coherence because the description of the disorder is presented to the reader at random; the writer has not taken a position from which to describe the disorder. The result is that the paragraph itself is disordered, as an analysis of the paragraph will quickly disclose. The second sentence, following the topic sentence, tells of the road and the weeds on each side of it. The third sentence talks about the barn. The fourth goes back to the road again. The fifth jumps to the house, and the sixth, to the pasture. The seventh returns to the house, and the eighth the road. The ninth describes the fence around the pasture; the tenth, the yard around the house; the eleventh, the barn; and the twelfth the pasture and cattle. Now, if the writer rearranges the sentences so that they present the objects on the farm as he sees them from a position of walking up the farm road to the house, he will have a more coherent paragraph.

The main characteristic of the little farm we had walked over was disorder. The winding, narrow road was bumpy and rough, and weeds grew rank and tall on each side of it. On one side of the road lay bundles of grain decaying from long exposure to wind, rain, and sunshine. On the other side, among the small, withered cotton plants, weeds sapped the soil. The fence around the pasture was badly in need of repairs. The wire was broken in many places, and the wooden posts, rotted at the ground, were supported by the rusty wire. In the pasture, diseased with weeds and underbrush, grazed thin, bony cattle revealing their need for more and better food and shelter. Near the barn stood a battered, unpainted tractor, plow, and rake. The barn itself lacked paint; its roof sagged and some of the shingles needed to be replaced. The house, too, needed paint and repairs. The steps and porch were rickety, and several of their boards were broken. A screen hung on one hinge. The broken window panes were mended with tin and boards. The yard was littered with rubbish—tin cans, broken bottles, and paper.

The paragraph now has a logical spatial order; it takes the reader from the road to either side of the road, to the pasture, and to the barn and house.

5. Coherence Through Related Sentence Patterns

A paragraph may be held together by repetition of sentence patterns within the paragraph. This method is a relatively difficult means of achieving coherence because it requires more care in designing sentences, but it is an effective means. Look at this paragraph.

> (1) To be genuinely civilized means to be able to walk straight and to live honorably without the props and crutches of one or another of the childish dreams which have so far supported men. (2) That such a life is likely to be ecstatically happy I will not claim. (3) But that it can be lived in quiet content, accepting resignedly what cannot be helped, not expecting the impossible, and thankful for small mercies, this I would maintain. (4) That it will be difficult for men in general to learn this lesson I do not deny. (5) But that it will be impossible I will not admit since so many have learned it already.[3]

Note that after the first sentence, the four remaining sentences are cast in the same form and are arranged in pairs, the second and third sentence constituting one pair, and the fourth and fifth sentences another. Look at the second sentence in the paragraph. It starts with a dependent clause *That such a life is likely to be ecstatically happy* and then finishes with a short independent clause *I will not claim.* The third sentence starts with a *but*, which ties it to the second sentence, and continues with exactly the same structure as that of the second sentence: *That it can be lived in quiet content . . . this I would maintain.* The first pair of sentences, joined together with *but*, is complete. The fourth sentence starts out exactly as the others, *That it will be difficult for men in general to learn this lesson*, and finishes with the identical short independent structure as the others, *I do not deny.* The fifth sentence begins with a *but*, which ties it to the fourth. Then comes the same type of dependent clause that has started the last three sentences, *that it will be impossible* followed by the independent clause, *I will not admit.*

Such a related sentence pattern is called parallel structure. It can be illustrated easily by a diagram.

> To be genuinely civilized means to be able to walk straight and to live honorably without the props and crutches of one or another of the childish dreams which have so far supported men.

3Stace, *ibid.*

That such a life is likely to be
    ecstatically happy
                      —I will not claim.

But

    that it can be lived in quiet
        content . . .
                      this I would maintain.

    That it will be difficult for men in
        general to learn this lesson
                      —I do not deny.

But

    that it will be impossible
                      —I will not admit
    since so many have learned it already.

6. Coherence Through Pronoun Reference

Look again at a paragraph quoted earlier, and another means of achieving coherence used in that paragraph becomes obvious.

> This doctrine of the relativity of morals, though it has recently received an impetus from the studies of anthropolgists, was thus really implicit in the whole scientific mentality. It is disastrous for morals because it destroys their entire traditional foundation. That is why philosophers who see the danger signals, from the time at least of Kant, have been trying to give to morals a new foundation, that is, a secular or nonreligious foundation. This attempt may very well be intellectually successful. Such a foundation, independent of the religious view of the world, might well be found. But the question is whether it can ever be a practical success, that is whether apart from its logical validity and its influence with intellectuals, it can ever replace among the masses of men the lost religious foundation. On that question hangs perhaps the future of civilization.[4]

Note the number of times the pronoun *it* has been circled and tied to the antecedent noun. Any pronoun is used for this purpose (*he*,

[4]Stace, *ibid.*

she, they, we, you, or any other case). This method is a simple means of maintaining coherence, and it is closely allied to consistency in point of view and to repetition of key words.

7. Coherence Through Transition Words

Probably the easiest, and most abused, method of pulling together the thought in a passage is through the use of transition words. Transition words or phrases bridge any gaps between sentences. They carry the reader from the thought of one sentence to that of another and indicate the relationship between the two sentences. An example of the way transition words work appeared earlier.

> John and Mary Vitek thought that under the circumstances there was only one course to take. *But* the young man on my left saw several alternatives.

The word that bridges the two sentences is *but.* The reader immediately expects a contrast to the thought of the previous sentence, and he proceeds without pause to see what that contrast is. This word has made a transition between the two sentences and has shown their relationship, one of contrast.

The English language furnishes a sufficient supply of transition words to express any relationship between two sentences. The diagram below illustrates the uses of the transition words.

transition word

Thought of Sentence 1		Thought of Sentence 2
	1. To indicate a conclusion or result.	
	2. To introduce an illustration.	
	3. To add to a thought.	
	4. To make a qualification or contrast.	

TO INDICATE A
CONCLUSION OR
RESULT

EXAMPLES

Therefore

As a result

Consequently

Accordingly

In other words

To sum up

Thus

Then

Hence

1. *Therefore*, his action can be justified by valid explanation.

2. *As a result*, hollow, vain aristocracies have been established on American campuses.

3. *Consequently*, the number of qualified voters remains small.

TO INTRODUCE AN
ILLUSTRATION

EXAMPLES

Thus

For example

For instance

To illustrate

Namely

1. *For example*, suppose I ask myself, "Will socialization ever come about?"

2. *For instance*, sophisticates can easily ridicule popular notions of government.

3. *Namely*, the men who complain the loudest are themselves the most guilty.

TO ADD A THOUGHT

EXAMPLES

Second

In the second place

Next

Likewise

Moreover

Again

In addition

Finally

Similarly

Further

1. *Similarly*, the German university can profit by adopting the American practice of letting the student do most of the talking.

2. *Second*, human happiness feeds itself on a multitude of minor illusions.

3. Then *again* we work and strive because of the illusions connected with fame.

4. *Moreover*, the child assumes an attitude that he knows is false.

TO MAKE A QUALIFICATION OR CONTRAST	EXAMPLES
On the other hand Nevertheless Still On the contrary By contrast However But Or Nor	1. He was not, *however*, completely qualified for the task he had undertaken. 2. The Dobu, *by contrast*, are portrayed as virtually a society of paranoids. 3. *Nevertheless*, these theories do contain real insights into the nature of value judgments. 4. *On the contrary*, one should not blindly assume that our birthrate will continue to climb.

The beginning writer will have to use some judgment to employ these transition words skillfully. Generally, he should keep two guidelines in mind.

1. *Use transition words sparingly.* The overuse of these words weakens writing style. Look at these sentences, for example:

> James went to the resort planning to stay three weeks, *but* he became disgusted after the first day. *Consequently*, he packed and went home.

The weakness in this example is indicated by the string of three independent clauses joined together in thought by transition words. It is much better to delete at least one transition word and change one of the independent clauses to dependent.

> James planned to stay three weeks at the resort, but after one day he became so disgusted that he packed and went home.

Here, the *consequently* has been dropped from the last sentence and the whole has been made into a dependent clause, *that he packed and went home.* This revision does make an acceptable sentence; but why not add some meaningful details, and make a good sentence out of it:

> Although James had planned a leisurely three weeks' stay at the resort, doing what he pleased when he pleased, he found himself caught up in so many planned activities—all arranged by a loud-

mouthed, back-slapping "entertainment" leader—that he packed his bags and left in disgust after one day.

2. *Use transition words to indicate logical relationships.* Consider this example:

> The College of Veterinary Medicine at Glory University is the only one in the state. *Therefore,* it is an excellent school.

In this example, the transition word *therefore* is not followed by a logical conclusion drawn from the evidence presented in the first sentence. Just because Glory University has the only College of Veterinary Medicine in the state, it does not necessarily follow that the college is excellent. This revision is much better:

> Glory University's College of Veterinary Medicine, the only one in the state, is an excellent school.

Or consider this sentence:

> Mary was healthy and robust, and she was born in Cincinnati in 1916.

The two parts of this sentence, *Mary was healthy and robust,* and *she was born in Cincinnati in 1916,* are not sufficiently related to be joined by a transition word. Apparently, the intent of this sentence is to comment on Mary's health for her age because her birth year is given. The place of her birth has nothing to do with any idea expressed in the sentence. The thought can be conveyed much better with a sentence such as this one:

> At fifty-one, Mary was healthy and robust.

Although the means of achieving coherence are considered separately in this chapter, it is not intended that only one of these means should be used in, say, one paragraph. The experienced writer may use several, even all, of them in any one paragraph to achieve the coherence he wants in his writing.

EXERCISES

A. Examine this paragraph to see if its coherence can be improved.
1 One of the fastest growing professions is college teaching. Its
2 growth has been high since World War II. Although there is a

3 scarcity of qualified applicants at this time, all indications point
4 to increasingly mounting needs. This year there are four mil-
5 lion college students. Estimates for 1973 are seven million
6 students. We now have 300,000 college teachers with an anti-
7 cipated need of 600,000 by 1978. Will these qualifications for
8 teachers be met by 1973?

Analysis:

1. Examine first the subjects of - the sentences. The subject of the first sentence (line 1) is *one*. The subject of the second sentence is *growth* (line 2). The subject of the third sentence is *indications* (line 3), of the fourth sentence is *students* (line 5), of the fifth *estimates* (line 5), of the sixth, *we* (line 6), of the seventh, *qualifications* (line 7)—for which the student writer of this paragraph apparently should have written *requirements* or *demands*. This examination indicates that a more consistent point of view should be maintained if this paragraph is to be coherent.

2. Examine the paragraph for other evidences of methods of maintaining coherence. There is some repetition of key words. *Growth* (line 2) repeats *growing* (line 1). *Teachers* (line 6) echoes *teaching* (line 1). *Students* (line 6) repeats *students* (line 5). There is no other use of this method, nor are there any transition words used in the paragraph. There is one pronoun reference. *Its* (line 1) refers to *college teaching* (line 1). There are no related sentence patterns and no spatial or chronological order (but neither of these last two would be appropriate here). Obviously, the coherence of this paragraph can be improved. Consider this revision.

1 The rapid increase in the number of students entering college
2 each year since World War II has caused college teaching to
3 become one of the fastest growing professions. This increase,
4 furthermore, has caused the profession to face a mounting
5 problem of finding enough qualified teachers to meet the
6 demand. At present, for example, the 300,000 college teachers
7 at work are not enough for the four million students in college,
8 and the number of qualified applicants for college teaching
9 positions is not sufficient to fill existing vacancies. How much
10 more difficult the problem will become in 1973 when at least
11 600,000 college teachers will be needed for the anticipated flood
12 of seven million students. Can the profession meet this demand
13 for college teachers by 1973?

Note the number of methods used to achieve coherence in this version. The subject of the first sentence, *increase*, is repeated as the subject of the second sentence (line 3). There are three transition words in the

paragraph—*furthermore* (line 4), *for example* (line 6), and *and* (line 8).
A number of key words are repeated several times. *Problem* (line 5) is
repeated in line 10. *Meet the demand* is a synonym for *problem* in this
paragraph. These words first appear in line 5 and are repeated in line 10.
Students (line 1) is repeated in line 7. *College teaching* and *teachers*
appear in lines 2, 5, 6, 8, 11, and 13. *Profession* (line 4) is repeated in
line 12. Obviously, the chief means of maintaining coherence in this paragraph is through repetition of key words. Of 126 words, 33, or 27.5 per
cent, are directly involved in maintaining the coherence of the paragraph.
This is not an unusually high percentage.

B. In the following paragraph, find the coherence devices and be able to
point them out. Lines of the paragraphs are numbered for your con-
venience.

1.

1 I have given the impression that the Farm was remote, but this
2 is not strictly true. Not half a mile on each side of us was
3 another farmhouse, and clustering near the one to the east
4 were three or four cottages. We formed, therefore, a little com-
5 munity, remote as such; in Doomsday Book, we had been
6 described as a hamlet. The nearest village was two or three
7 miles away, but to the south, so that it did not count for much
8 until we began to go to school, which was not until toward
9 the end of the period of which I write. Northward our farm
10 road ran through two fields and then joined the highroad run-
11 ning east and west; but eastward this road soon turned into a
12 road running north and south, down which we turned north-
13 ward again, to the Church five miles away, and to Kirby, our
14 real metropolis, six miles away.[5]

2.

1 The farmhouse was a square stone box with a roof of vivid red
2 tiles; its front was to the south, and warm enough to shelter
3 some apricot trees against the wall. But there was no traffic
4 that way: All our exits and entrances were made on the north
5 side, through the kitchen and I think even our grandest visitors
6 did not disdain that approach. Why should they? On the left
7 as they entered direct into the kitchen was an old ash dresser;
8 on the right a large open fireplace, with a great iron kettle
9 hanging from the reckan, and an oven to the near side of it.
10 A long deal table, glistening with a honey gold sheen from
11 much scrubbing, filled the far side of the room; long benches
12 ran down each side of it. The floor was flagged with stone neatly

[5]Herbert Read, *The Innocent Eye*. Copyright 1947 by Herbert Read. Reprinted by permission of Harold Ober Associates Incorporated.

13 outlined with a border of some softer yellow stone, rubbed on
14 after every washing. Sides of bacon and plum dusky hams hung
15 from the beams of the wooden ceiling.[6]

3.

1 By day it was the scene of intense bustle. The kitchenmaid was
2 down by five o'clock to light the fire; the laborers crept down
3 in stockinged feet and drew on their heavy boots; they lit
4 candles in their horn lanthorns and went out to the cattle.
5 Breakfast was at seven, dinner at twelve, tea at five. Each
6 morning of the week had its appropriate activity: Monday was
7 washing day, Tuesday ironing, Wednesday and Saturday baking,
8 Thursday "turning out" upstairs and churning, Friday "turning
9 out" downstairs. Every day there was the milk to skim in the
10 dairy—the dairy was to the left of the kitchen and as big as any
11 room in the house.[7]

4.

1 At dinner, according to the time of the year, there would be
2 from five to seven farm laborers, the two servant girls, and the
3 family, with whom, for most of the time, there was a governess
4 —a total of from ten to fifteen mouths to feed every day. The
5 bustle reached its height about midday; the men would come
6 in and sit on the dresser, swinging their legs impatiently; when
7 the food was served, they sprang to the benches and ate in solid
8 gusto, like animals. They disappeared as soon as the pudding
9 had been served, some to smoke a pipe in the saddle room,
10 others to do work which could not wait. Then all the clatter
11 of washing up rose and subsided. More peaceful occupations
12 filled the afternoon. The crickets began to sing in the hearth.
13 The kettle boiled for tea. At nightfall a candle was lit, the
14 foreman or the shepherd sat smoking in the armchair at the
15 fireside end of the table. The latch clicked as the others came
16 in one by one and went early up to bed.[8]

5.

1 Many critics of our society have said that we lack standards.
2 This has been said so often by preachers and by the makers of
3 commencement addresses that we have almost stopped asking
4 what, if anything, it means to say that our society "lacks
5 standards." But that we do lack standards for welfare and stan-
6 dards for education is obvious. Welfare turns into vulgar
7 materialism because we have no standard by which to measure

[6]*Ibid.*
[7]*Ibid.*
[8]*Ibid.*

8 it. Education fails because it also refuses to face the responsibil-
9 ity of saying in what education consists. Both tend to become
10 merely what people seem to want.[9]

6.

1 Duration is not the only political virtue, but it is a virtue.
2 Constitutions, by their name and function, can be deemed
3 successes only if they last long enough to give stability to the
4 political life of the society they are supposed to serve. The
5 American Constitution passes that test. But a constitution can
6 survive in a form that makes it less and less adequate for the
7 needs of the society it purports to serve, and either that society
8 is cribbed, cabined and confined, held within an armor that
9 forbids adaptation or growth, or the constitution is disregarded
10 and the true political forces grow up beside it, paying only lip
11 service to the antique and obsolete forms, as Prussia grew up in
12 the carapace of the constitution of the Holy Roman Empire
13 of the German People. That has not happened in the United
14 States. The Constitution is still at the center of American gov-
15 ernment and politics. It must be reckoned with every day by
16 the President, by the Congress, by the Courts, by labor, by
17 business. It has proved sufficiently adaptable to permit the
18 expansion of the thin line of newly emancipated colonies
19 along the Atlantic seaboard to the Pacific, the multiplication
20 of the population fifty-fold and the extension of the armed
21 power of the United States almost around the globe. It has
22 permitted the growth of these remote and, in 1789, impov-
23 erished colonies to an economic power and a material wealth
24 unprecedented in human history. And it has done all this with-
25 out distorting its fundamental character or denying the political
26 theories and system of values on which it was based.[10]

7.

1 Studies serve for delight, for ornament, and for ability. Their
2 chief use for delight, is in privateness and retiring; for orna-
3 ment, is in discourse; and for ability, is in the judgment and
4 disposition of business. For expert men can execute, and per-
5 haps judge of particulars, one by one; but the general counsels,
6 and the plots and marshalling of affairs, come best from those
7 that are learned. To spend too much time in studies is sloth;
8 to use them too much for ornament is affectation; to make

[9]Joseph Wood Krutch, "Life, Liberty, and the Pursuit of Welfare," *Saturday Evening Post*, July 15, 1961. Copyright 1961 by The Curtis Publishing Company. Reprinted by permission of the author.

[10]D. W. Brogan, *Politics in America*. Copyright 1954 by D. W. Brogan. Used by permission of Harper & Row, Publishers, Inc., and of Hamish Hamilton Ltd.

9 judgment wholly by their rules, is the humour of a scholar.
10 They perfect nature, and are perfected by experience: for
11 natural abilities are like natural plants, that need pruning by
12 study; and studies themselves do give forth directions too much
13 at large, except they be bounded in by experience. Crafty men
14 contemn studies, simple men admire them, and wise men use
15 them; for they teach not their own use; but that is a wisdom
16 without them, and above them, won by observation. Read not
17 to contradict and confute; nor to believe and take for granted;
18 not to find talk and discourse; but to weigh and consider. Some
19 books are to be tasted, others to be swallowed, and some few
20 to be chewed, and digested; that is, some books are to be read
21 only in parts; others to be read, but not curiously; and some
22 few to be read wholly, and with diligence and attention. . . .[11]

[11]Francis Bacon, "Of Studies." Many editions.

Writing Paragraphs

4

You have learned about the organization of the five-hundred-word paper, about the framing of a thesis statement, and about unity and coherence; the next step is to learn to write the paragraphs that make up the paper. You will be concerned with two types of paragraphs—the introductory and the developmental. The first is fairly simple; for the second, however, you will learn to develop paragraphs by use of detail, by use of definition, by use of illustration and example, by use of comparison and contrast, and by use of reason. But, first, the introductory paragraph.

INTRODUCTORY PARAGRAPH

The opening paragraph of the five-hundred-word paper has two purposes: It introduces the subject of the paper, and in the last sentence of the paragraph, it specifically presents the thesis statement to be established in the developmental paragraphs that follow. The introductory paragraph need be only about fifty to seventy-five words, a sufficient length to establish the subject of the paper. A paper longer than five hundred words might require a longer introduction reviewing the background of the subject to be discussed. In five-hundred-word papers, however, there is no space for lengthy exploration of the subject; you must get the statement of your subject out of the way as efficiently as possible. Then, you can use the allotted space to best advantage in developing and supporting your thesis.

An introductory paragraph starts with a broad, general statement introducing the subject of the paper, and then qualifies this subject statement by narrowing it to the specific thesis statement of the paper. This construction can best be seen in the following diagram.

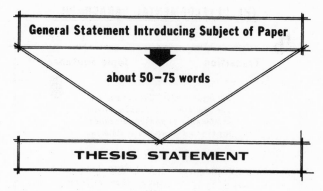

Now, look at an example of a student's introductory paragraph that follows this pattern.

> Women find various reasons for marrying: because it is convenient, or desirable, or highly acceptable to society, or sometimes even because it is necessary. But whatever her reasons, I contend that a woman should not marry a college student.

Note that this paragraph starts with a general statement about the reasons women marry and then in thirty-nine words reduces this statement to a specific thesis statement to be established in the remainder of the paper. It wastes no time in getting to the main business of the paper, supporting the thesis statement in the developmental paragraphs.

Here is another example that does the same thing in seventy-eight words.

> High school students, usually not avid readers of comic books, sometimes resort to substituting "classic" comic books for required reading. Basically honest, many of these students, under pressure of heavy assignments and extracurricular activities, think of the classic comic as merely a short cut in completing an assignment. Although these students may be able to write a plot summary from their reading of the classic comic, they are cheating themselves when they take this easy way out.

DEVELOPMENTAL PARAGRAPHS

The developmental paragraphs are the meat of your paper. They present the evidence you have for believing in your thesis statement, and you must put effort and thought into writing them. Again, a diagram explains the developmental paragraph.

THE DEVELOPMENTAL PARAGRAPH

Transition	Topic Sentence

Detail, definition, illustration, comparison, contrast, reason, or any combination of methods establishing the topic sentence as valid.

(About 150 to 200 words)

MAINTAIN UNITY: Stay on the single subject given in the topic sentence.

MAINTAIN COHERENCE: Use transitional devices to relate sentences.

In this diagram, the space representing the first sentence in the paragraph is divided. The first part is labeled Transition. It indicates that a word, phrase, clause, or sentence should ordinarily be used in this position to provide a connection between this paragraph and the preceding one. The second part is the topic sentence, which leads into the paragraph. For example, look at this opening sentence:

> I am arguing, *then*, that there are *two readers distinguishable* in every literary experience. . . .

Then is a transition word that suggests a summing up and a continuation of the thought of the preceding paragraph. The *two readers* in the last part of the sentence are to be explained in the remainder of the paragraph.

> *I have given the impression that the Farm was remote,* but *this is not strictly true.*

The first part of this beginning sentence points back to the preceding paragraph. The last part points forward to the remainder of the paragraph by announcing its topic.

> Closely associated with *this distinction* between author and speaker, *there is another and less familiar distinction* to be made. . . .

This distinction in the first of the sentence is obviously the subject of the preceding paragraph. *Another and less familiar distinction* is the subject of this paragraph.

> Although fraternity *expenses* are less hindrance to affluent members, the society *interferes* indiscriminately *with the studies* of its members. . . .

Here *expenses* refers to the subject of the preceding paragraph; *interferes with studies* is the subject of the paragraph the sentence introduces.

These sentences all demonstrate transitional techniques necessary for the reader's easy progress from the main point of one paragraph to the main point of the next. Be careful to use such techniques so that your whole paper, as well as your paragraphs, may have coherence.

PARAGRAPH DEVELOPMENT BY USE OF DETAIL

Have a look at two students' paragraphs and the discussion of them that follows. Here is the first one.

> People who buy foreign economy cars are not getting what they think they are paying for. Foreign cars are not really any more economical to operate than are American cars. Those who talk about how good foreign cars are simply do not know what they are talking about. They should spend more time studying the durability record of American cars than just thinking about gas mileage. Many small foreign cars are worn out after 50,000 miles and have to be replaced. American cars will run much longer than this. So foreign cars are not good buys.

This paragraph was written by a student who had been assigned a paper to write in class at the beginning of the semester. After completing this paragraph and making several attempts to continue writing the paper, the student appealed to his instructor for help. What, he wanted to know, could he say next? The instructor explained that the broad ideas in the paragraph were undeveloped and that the student needed to use detail to support his ideas and to convince his reader. Consider, for instance, the general statement that foreign cars are not any more economical to operate than are American cars: What detailed facts could the student present to make this statement more than simply an assertion that it is true? Without the facts, thousands of foreign car drivers may not agree with him.

Here is the second one.

> The adoption of medicare can cause serious damage to our system of free enterprise and private medicine. It would ruin many medicinal producing corporations and cause unemployment for thousands of workers. The control of medicine would pass from the doctors to the government. Our system of medicine has worked for over 180 years. Why destroy it now with medicare? Why take from the skilled hands of our doctors and give to untrained "butchers" of socialized medicine? This can not be allowed in the United States. Medicare must not be allowed to destroy our democratic system.

This student apparently feels quite strongly about his subject, so strongly, in fact, that he has let the discussion get out of hand. Personal belief in a subject is not enough to convince others. And no matter how the reader personally feels about medicare, he certainly must recognize this piece of writing as ranting and fanatic opinion unsupported by evidence. Logically, the paragraph is impossible. It equates free enterprise, private medicine, and democracy. These are not interdependent, as can be easily shown, and one does not necessarily collapse when one of the others does. How, for instance, can medicare ruin *medicinal producing corporations* and cause unemployment? Why are the practitioners of socialized medicine called *butchers*? Are medicare and socialized medicine the same thing, as this paragraph asserts? How can medicare *destroy our democratic system*? How will it damage *free enterprise*? All these questions are unanswered, and we must only conclude that this student needs to support his opinions with detail.

But he needs to learn more than this. He needs to learn to

Use detailed *FACTS*:
1. To support *ideas*.
2. To support *judgments* or *opinions*.

And he needs an understanding of the terms *fact, judgment, opinion,* and *inference*.

By definition, a *FACT* is a verifiable statement, something everyone will agree to. For instance, the following sentences are all fact.

1. Yesterday there was a car wreck on Highway 6 about three miles south of the city limits. (This statement is easily verifiable by the police or the newspapers. Anyone will accept the validity of either source.)

2. The Weather Bureau reported that 3.00 inches of rain fell on the city yesterday. (Here the question of fact is not whether 3.00 inches of rain fell but whether the Weather Bureau reported that. Again, this fact is easily checked in the newspaper or at the Bureau.)

3. There are sidewalks on each side of the street. (Anyone who questions this statement can check it simply by looking at the street. Probably, no one would want to question it.)

4. In 1960, Texas had a population of 9,579,677. (Easily verified by the government census reports for 1960.)

5. John Jones told me that he saw a leopard change its spots. (Here again the question is not whether John Jones saw a leopard change its spots but whether he told me that he saw it. As long as John Jones will admit that he told it, the statement is verifiable. If he will not, the question must be resolved by the reliability and reputation of the two people involved.)

An *OPINION* is a conclusion or conviction formed about any matter. It is, of course, based on evidence, as all conclusions or convictions are, but the evidence can be logically sound or logically fallacious. An opinion is open to dispute and is not a soundly proved matter. It should be based on factual evidence, and a person expressing an opinion should be able to support it with fact and sound logic. Or he should have such a reputation for his experience with the subject and his knowledge of it that he is recognized as an authority. Without either fact or authority, an opinion holds little weight in any discussion.

Perhaps most often, human nature being what it is, opinions appear as judgments. A *JUDGMENT* is a statement indicating approval or disapproval of objects, happenings, persons, or ideas. Judgment, a form of opinion, is also based on some kind of evidence, but particular care must be taken in forming judgments and in expressing them. For instance, suppose your family bought a house from a real estate agent named John Jones and that before you made the down payment he promised to put a new roof on the house. When no workmen appeared to start work on the roof and you asked Jones when he was going to order the roof put on, he denied making any such promise. Your first reaction would probably be "John Jones is a crook," and you might make this statement to your friends. But wait. Even though Jones has wronged you, to call him a crook is to say that he has been a crook and always will be a crook in business dealings. On the basis of this one example only, such a judgment is hardly justified. About all you can say is that in this situation you think Jones dealt with you unethically. Or suppose you bought a Waumpum car two years ago and that you have now driven it for 75,000 miles with only a few minor repairs. You might well say, "The Waumpum is an excellent car." Yet the fact may be that yours is the only Waumpum to go over 50,000 miles without a motor overhaul. Again, on the basis of experience with one car of one model, such a judgment is not justified. Judgments and opinions such as these should not appear in your papers unless they are firmly and soundly supported by factual evidence.

Imagine yourself in a situation such as this one: You observe a woman you have seen many times before, and you turn to your friend and say, "There goes that wealthy woman I see all over town." Your friend says, "Really? How do you know she is wealthy?" "Well," you reply, "she wears obviously expensive clothes, she drives a large, late model car, and she lives in a house that anyone would call a mansion." "That doesn't prove anything," says the friend. "She may just be deep in debt." Your friend would be right; you have not proved your point. But you did form an inference about the woman. An *INFERENCE* is a guess about the unknown based on the known. But an inference is not necessarily a valid conclusion, because there are usually other guesses that may be just as logically derived from the evidence. For instance, suppose in the middle of a classroom lecture the student sitting next to you suddenly bangs his book closed, grimaces, rises and stomps out of the room, slamming the door behind him. You might say to yourself, "Something the professor said made him angry." But again you might be wrong. The student may have had a sudden and uncontrollable stomach cramp from something he ate for lunch, and it became imperative for him to leave the room at once. There are other possible inferences to be drawn from the student's actions. Inferences cannot, therefore, be positively stated as if they were valid conclusions and absolute truth.

EXERCISES

A. Identify the following statements as fact, judgment, or inference.
   1. My history teacher has asked me a question in class every day for the past two weeks.
   2. Don't take that history course—it's tough.
   3. The referee penalized our team seventy-five yards in that game with Primitive University.
   4. We lost that game to the referee.
   5. We would have won that game with Primitive University if we had not been penalized so much.
   6. That referee was no good.
   7. Only twenty-five percent of that professor's students passed the last examination. It's time for an investigation of his teaching methods.
   8. Termites have damaged the floor joists in that house.
   9. I studied everything and went to class every time, but I still didn't pass because the teacher doesn't like me.
   10. That's the worst teacher I ever had.

B. The first statement in this group is fact and the others are based on it. Identify them as judgment or inference.
   1. There is a six-foot fence around their house.
   2. They don't want people to visit them.
   3. Their house looks like a prison.
   4. They want privacy in their home.
   5. There must be something wrong with those people.
   6. Those people are crazy.
   7. They must have something to hide.
   8. I don't like that house with its high fence.

C. List the inferences that might be drawn from these sets of circumstances.
   1. He was weaving as he walked along. He staggered several times. He suddenly sat down on the curb and held his head in his hands.
   2. The man ran from the store in great haste. He jumped in his car and sped away. The store's owner ran out on the curb and shouted something after him.
   3. After dinner she went straight to her room, took out paper and pen and spent four busy hours writing her English paper. She received a failing grade on it.

4. Everyone must be convinced by now that cigarette smoking does contribute to the high incidence of lung cancer. Yet the rate of cigarette consumption in the United States increases each year.
5. While the population of the United States has been increasing, church attendance has been decreasing.

D. Select from each of the lists you have written for Exercise C the inference you think is likely to be the most valid, and indicate your reasons for thinking so.

Using Specific Details

Now that you have learned not to use opinion, judgment, or inference as fact, you will also learn to distinguish between the specific and the general in developing paragraphs by use of detail, and you will want to learn to use the *SPECIFIC* rather than the general in supporting ideas, opinions, or judgments.

The *GENERAL* includes *all* a class, type, or group. For example *structure* is a general term, because there are several types of structures. The *SPECIFIC*, on the other hand, refers to a *particular* in a class, type, or group. A building, a bridge, a television transmitting antenna, or a radar tower are each a particular of the general class, structure. Therefore, *building* is more specific than *structure*, because it is only one member of the whole class. In the same way, *box* is more specific than *container*, because a box is only one type of container. *Horse* is more specific than *vertebrate*; *boat*, more specific than *vehicle*; *meat*, more specific than *food*; and *furniture*, more specific than *household goods*.

But all these terms can be made yet more specific. *Building*, even though it is a type of structure, is still a general term that can be divided into types. A house, a service station, a garage, or a greenhouse can all be called buildings and are, therefore, more specific than *building*. Again, a filly is a type of horse, a wooden crate is a type of box, a chair is a type of furniture, beef is a type of meat, and a kayak is a type of boat. These terms can be made still more specific by reference to building material, color, location, shape, or size. For instance, *brick house* is more specific than *house*, and *red brick house* is still more specific. *The red brick house on Lincoln Street* will specify even further by pointing to a particular house.

Similarly, beef is a type of meat, steak is a type of beef, sirloin steak is a type of steak, and grilled sirloin steak is one type of sirloin steak. And the sirloin can be made more specific by describing its appearance: *grilled sirloin steak, charred on the outside, raw within.*

EXERCISES

I. Select from the following groups the most specific in each group.

    A. (1) dog (2) mammal (3) large bird dog (4) setter (5) canine

    B. (1) a great boy (2) a witty and charming boy (3) a boy with a top-notch personality (4) a wonderful boy to know

    C. (1) John and Mary served a large quantity of food. (2) Their table literally groaned with an abundance of viands. (3) They served a quantity of foods suitable for the Thanksgiving season and tempting to the most jaded palate. (4) In the center of their table was a large baked turkey surrounded by dishes of cranberry sauce, sweet potatoes, giblet gravy, rolls, and pumpkin pie. (5) Their cuisine was liberally illustrated by the delicious and nourishing products of culinary art distributed on the table in great number.

    Answers: In *A, setter* is the most specific term, because it names the type of dog involved. In this group, *mammal* is the most general term, followed by *canine, dog,* and *large bird dog.* If you picked *witty and charming boy* in *B* as the most specific in this group, you were correct. In fact, of the choices here, this is the only one that gives any specific information about the boy. *C* is easy. Number 4 is the only one in this group that tells specifically what food was on the table.

II. Select the most specific from each of these groups.

    A. (1) mosquito (2) blood-sucking insect (3) creature (4) invertebrate (5) insect with two wings

    B. (1) man (2) person (3) individual (4) student (5) one

    C. (1) a building with an established place in the history of one of our largest states (2) a historical shrine revered by Texans (3) an old stone mission where, in 1836, Santa Anna's 4,000 Mexican troops, after a thirteen day siege, defeated and slaughtered Colonel Travis' Texas garrison of 180 men (4) a rambling structure, once a church, where Texas history was made (5) an old mission where the Mexican forces massacred the defending Texans

D. (1) He wore a battered brown derby, a new light-orange sport jacket, red slacks, frayed white spats, and black shoes. (2) He was extremely oddly dressed. (3) His hat and his spats were certainly from another era, but his coat and slacks were modern, although their colors were so loud they hurt the eyes of the onlooker. (4) No piece of his clothing matched any other piece. (5) He wore an old derby, a coat that clashed sharply with the color of his slacks, spats, and shoes.

E. (1) The book ends with a scene of mounting interest and excitement that leaves the reader sitting on the edge of his chair. (2) The ending of the book is simply magnificent in the gripping realism of its final scene. (3) At the end of the book, after Jack's followers, now complete savages, have set fire to the island and have hunted Ralph down to kill him, the reader understands with almost unbearable clarity the cruelty inherent in all mankind. (4) At the end of the book, after a series of highly interesting scenes, the reader is brought face to face with certain facts about modern life.

Using Details in Paragraph Development

In diagram form, here is the paragraph developed through use of detail.

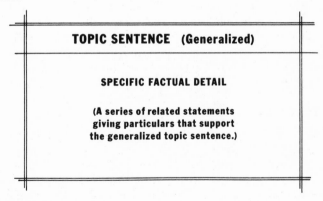

TOPIC SENTENCE (Generalized)

SPECIFIC FACTUAL DETAIL

(A series of related statements giving particulars that support the generalized topic sentence.)

Here is an example of a paragraph developed through use of details taken from the work of a successful writer.

Freeman Halverson is tall, fast on his feet, and works hard. On his slender shoulders are laid many of the responsibilities of the little community. He is postmaster, storekeeper, driver of the school bus. He is chairman of the community study group, head of the newly organized conservation unit, president of the state alfalfa seed growers' association, editor of the Hub News. He is on the citizens' advisory board of the state agricultural college. He leads the Lonepine band. At times he trains the girls' chorus. And then toward the evening he plays the clarinet at home in the family ensemble.[1]

This paragraph establishes the pointer in the topic sentence, *responsibilities*, by detailing the duties Freeman Halverson carries in the community. When the reader finishes the paragraph, he can only agree with the author that Halverson does, indeed, carry many of the responsibilities of the community.

Read this paragraph. You can recognize it as coming from the same work.

> Freeman Halverson is the downtown population of Lonepine, he and perhaps Ted Van der Ende, the cheesemaker. Freeman Halverson is postmaster and the owner and operator of the general store. His place is the rendezvous. *The post office is on one side of the room.* For a time the public library also was housed here. Below are freeze lockers. The butcher shop with its big refrigerator is at the back. In *this* building with its somewhat informal front porch may be bought a *wide variety of goods. Sales* are announced in the weekly *news sheet,* and the prices paid for local produce are revised to suit the season.[2]

You have already seen how effectively this author uses detail to support his ideas; therefore, you might be immediately suspicious of this paragraph, particularly if you examined the italicized parts. These parts indicate where detail might be used to good effect. The fact is that the author did not write this paragraph in quite this way. He supplied the needed details. Look at the way he actually wrote it. The details he used are italicized.

> Freeman Halverson is the downtown population of Lonepine, he and perhaps Ted Van der Ende, the cheesemaker. Freeman Halverson is posmaster and the owner and operator of the general store. His place is the rendezvous. The tiny post office, *not much larger than a telephone booth,* is on *the drygoods side* of the *big* room. For a time the public library also was housed here. Below

[1]Baker Brownell, *The Human Comedy* (Harper & Brothers, 1950). Reprinted by permission of Harper & Row, Publishers, Inc.
[2]*Ibid.*

are freeze lockers. The butcher shop with its big refrigerator is at the back. In this *rambling frame* building with its somewhat informal front porch may be bought a *modern cream separator* or *a pair of overalls, a pound of cheese or a tube of lipstick, a silken, western neckerchief, a saddle or a pound of old fashioned chocolate creams. Brisk bargains* are announced in the weekly *mimeographed* sheet of *news* and *market items,* and the prices paid for local *eggs* and *poultry, vegetables, seeds, potatoes,* and *fruit* are revised to suit the season.[3]

Now the paragraph is specific in its detail, and the reader has a much better idea of the effect the author intended to create.

Here are some students' paragraphs developed through the use of detail. Examine them carefully, for they will serve as models for your writing:

The catcher is the "quarterback" of baseball. In effect, he runs the team. He is the only man who sees every player on the field and observes every move that takes place. He calls the pitches by giving signals to the pitcher. Sometimes he directs much of the defensive play by stationing the players in key spots and by directing the moves against the opposition. He is the one player on the team who can never for a moment relax, whether his team is in the field or at bat. He must know wind directions in every ball park, and he must study the opposing batteries, the mental condition of his own pitcher, and the spacing of his fielders. And he must watch runners on base, keeping track of the tactical situation and seeing that the rest of the team knows it also.

This paragraph uses the details of the catcher's job to establish the point that the catcher "runs" the baseball team. Enough detail is included to make the point of the topic sentence quite clear. Here is another example paragraph.

We could not use the table he showed us. The wood was rough and saw-marked, and the finish was dull and spotty. The top was marked with several cigarette burns, although a label on the bottom promised that it was fireproof. Stains and scuffs also marred the top. The construction was poor; the joints were ill-fitted, and one leg was held on by a wire. The metal cap on one of the legs, provided originally to protect the carpet, was missing, and the drawer, which had no handle, could not be opened more than three inches. Furthermore, the table was too long for practical use and too wide to be easily moved through the door.

[3]*Ibid.*

In this paragraph, abundant detail is used to support the point of the topic sentence: The table was beyond use.

Here is a paragraph written by a student in business administration with previous business experience.

> Few people know the significant criteria that a financial manager must consider in devising a company's financial plan. He must keep abreast of the general level of business activity to determine the company's needs for assets and funds. To operate efficiently he must interpret and use money and capital markets to the fullest extent. He must know the effects of tax rates and whether an increase or decrease in the tax rates will raise or lower the desirability of indebtedness. He must cope with seasonal and cyclical variations in business activity. To as great a degree as possible, he must know the nature and effects of competitors. He must use regulations and customs to the best practical extent. He must know the credit standing of his company and strive to keep it as high as possible.

The next paragraph was written by an expert bowler, a student who gave bowling lessons at the Student Union lanes.

> Although the experts all claim that proper form is the most important aspect of good bowling, consistency is the real secret for a bowler. The bowler may push the ball away too fast, but if he does it the same way every time, his game will not suffer. He may backswing too high or too low, but if the ball reaches the identical spot in the backswing arc in each delivery, the high score compiled for each game will not reveal the weakness. He may take more or fewer steps than the recommended four, as long as he takes the same number in each approach. The bowler may even commit the unpardonable sin of releasing the ball while on the wrong foot, provided he can do it exactly the same way every time. In other words, the bowler can do everything "wrong" and still be an expert bowler, if he will do it "wrong" consistently.

This paragraph makes its point about consistency being the secret of good bowling by detailing the things a bowler may do wrong consistently but still bowl well.

This paragraph was written by a young high school teacher who had returned to college after teaching for a year on a temporary certificate.

> Although many people think the work of a public school teacher is easy, the school teacher actually has the responsibility of many jobs. Before school opens in the fall, the teacher must attend meetings every day, sometimes for as long as a week, in preparation for

the fall semester. During the semester, the teacher has official meetings, such as those for the faculty and the PTA, that he must
attend. He is expected to sponsor clubs, coach athletics, and help
promote such fund raising activities as carnivals. He has monitorial
duties to perform when he is not in class. But, of course, his primary
job is teaching. He must teach about five classes a day and sometimes conduct an additional study hall. In preparation for instruct-
ing his classes, the teacher spends about five to six hours a week
preparing materials and reading to supplement textbooks. Still he
must spend some of his "off" hours at school helping individual
students having personal problems or difficulty learning the material.
Furthermore, he must grade papers, evaluate the students' progress,
make reports of various kinds, and even interview the parents of
his students. But this is not all. To keep up with new teaching
methods and programs the teacher himself must often go to school
in the summer and attend conventions. And occasionally, he must
take part in such community affairs as luncheons and civic organiza-
tions.

After reading this paragraph with its detailing of the teacher's
duties, anyone must agree with the point stated in the topic sentence.

Summary

1. Start a beginning paragraph with a general statement and
narrow it to the thesis statement.

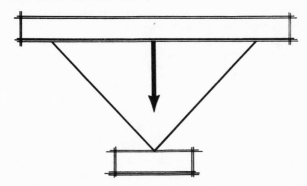

2. Learn to distinguish:

FACT: a statement that is verifiable.

INFERENCE: a guess based on known fact.
    (May be valid but may not be)

OPINION: a conclusion, or conviction, established about a matter.

(May be based on no fact)

JUDGMENT: statement made of approval or disapproval.
(May be based on no fact or insufficient fact)

3. In supporting inferences, opinions, or judgments (generalizations), use *specific facts.*

GENERAL: a broad term covering many particulars (the whole).

SPECIFIC: a narrow term specifying a particular (a small part of the whole).

THESIS STATEMENTS and TOPIC SENTENCES are supported by related, factual, specific statements.

EXERCISES

A. List the details that might be used to support five of the statements below.
   1. The college student's life is difficult.
   2. A man needs to be married.
   3. Car manufacturers are (are not) meeting human needs in automobile safety.
   4. Each year television increases (or decreases) its cultural impact.
   5. Men spend too much money on dates.
   6. Sunday dinner proved again that Mama was no cook.
   7. The clock Mary Jane brought home from the discount house was no bargain.
   8. The interior decorator left nothing in the dining room as it had been before.
   9. Graduation exercises were not boring that year.
   10. We didn't know where to start on the cleanup job.

B. Rewrite these paragraphs and supply appropriate, specific detail at the italicized points. Freely add and change material that is here.
   1. He stared at the carnival booth as if hypnotized. From it issued *highly amplified sounds* that almost overcame him with their intensity. Its *many* shelves were stacked with *a variety of flashy goods. Some men stood* at the booth's counter intently concentrating on looping hoops over a *stick some feet away. A few boys* chased each other through the *people* standing at the booth.

2. They entertained the *group of visitors* as best they could with such short notice. First, there was a *lunch outdoors,* followed by a long walk through *interesting gardens* of the city. After resting, the visitors were taken to *a local museum* where they were shown *relics of bygone days,* and in the evening they saw *a stage show of their choice.* At the end of the planned activities, the host took the entire group to his home, where they were joined by *friends of the hosts* for a *party to climax the delightful visit.*

3. *A manufacturing firm nearby* went all out to advertise their products and to establish goodwill in the community at the same time. They ran a contest in the spring that offered a *costly grand prize* for the best slogan in praise of their products. In the winter, they offered an all-expense-paid trip *to the South* for the merchant who arranged the Ideal Display of the firm's products. For the consumer who could think up original ideas for putting the firm's merchandise to use, *there was a reward.* The community showed its appreciation *in many ways.*

4. The bride-to-be found it difficult to display all her lovely gifts in her parents' *small* home. Relatives from out of town had sent *lightweight but expensive knickknacks.* All these had arrived early and seemed to get choice spots in the living room. *Gifts of bedding and kitchenware* from nearby kinfolk covered the dining table and took all the space *on other furniture* in the dining room. Chums in her own age group had sent the bride more *"mod" gifts,* and these took over the TV room and what shelf space *there was in the house. Her gift from the groom's parents,* the one she treasured most highly of all, because of its resale value, the bride kept in her purse and brought it out for frequent praise from *interested parties.*

C. Write three paragraphs developed through the use of detail, using three of the lists composed in Exercise A.

PARAGRAPH DEVELOPMENT BY USE OF DEFINITION

Before studying the means of using definition in paragraph development, read through this paragraph, a definition of *democracy*, written by the well-known historian Carl Becker. It will give you a good idea of what it means to use definition.

In this antithesis there are, however, certain implications, always tacitly understood, which give a more precise meaning to the term democracy. Peisistratus, for example, was supported by a majority of the people, but his government was never regarded as a democracy for all that. Caesar's power derived from a popular mandate, conveyed through established republican forms, but this did not make his government any less a dictatorship. Napoleon called his government a democratic empire, but no one, least of all Napoleon himself, doubted that he had destroyed the last vestiges of the democratic republic. Since the Greeks first used the term, the essential test of democratic government has always been this: the source of political authority must be and remain in the people and not in the ruler. A democratic government has always meant one in which the citizens, or a sufficient number of them to represent more or less effectively the common will, freely act from time to time, and accordingly to established forms, to appoint or recall the magistrates and to enact or revoke the laws by which the community is governed. This I take to be the meaning which history has impressed upon the term democracy as a form of government.[4]

This paragraph starts with a conventional topic sentence using *implications* as the pointer to give the paragraph unity. It explores these implications chronologically by use of examples starting with the Greeks (Peisistratus) and ending with France's Napoleonic Empire. When the paragraph comes to a statement of the principal implication, which is Becker's one-sentence definition of democracy, it maintains coherence by reference to the Greeks, mentioned early in the paragraph. After the one-sentence definition, . . . *the source of political authority must be and remain in the people and not in the ruler*, the paragraph explains in more detail what this definition means. In the final sentence, the paragraph declares that this is the meaning of democracy that Mr. Becker is to use throughout his book, and the reader need have no misunderstanding of what he means when he uses the word.

As Becker has done in this paragraph, you must also define the terms you use in writing, if there is any chance that your reader may use a different meaning from the one you intend. Many a verbal argument has ended with some such statement, as "It has become obvious that we are not defining our terms in the same way, and I won't accept your definitions." This usually ends the argument, because without acceptable definitions there is no real communication. One group talks about one thing and the other group is arguing another, although they seem to be talking about the

[4]Carl Becker, *Modern Democracy.* Copyright 1954 by Yale University Press. Used by permission of Yale University Press.

same subject. Throughout one presidential campaign, for instance, there was a running argument over whether the United States is a republic or a democracy, but nowhere in the campaign were these two terms satisfactorily defined, nor was the distinction between the two made clear. Consequently, the argument carried little weight with the voting public. So make the meaning of the terms you use in writing clear to the reader. Defining terms will not necessarily make the reader agree with you, but without adequate definitions, he cannot tell what you are saying.

When you decide a term needs defining, you will not want to copy verbatim the dictionary definition and use it in your paper with some phrase as "Webster defines socialism as. . . ." Such a practice defeats your purpose, which is to make clear the exact meaning *you* are attaching to a word. You can devise your own definitions. There are five methods of doing so.

1. Classification
2. Synonyms
3. Enumeration
4. Examples or illustrations
5. Function

Consider these methods one at a time.

Definition by Classification

This is also called the Aristotelian method, and it is the one most often found in dictionaries. Its use is quite simple and involves only two steps:

1. Place the word to be defined in its family (genus).
2. Differentiate the word from all others in its family.

For instance, if you wanted to define the relatively simple word *bridge* (to indicate that you do not mean the card game or a part of the nose or of a pair of spectacles or an arch to raise the strings of a musical instrument or a raised platform on a ship or a transition in music), you would first place the word in its family:

A bridge is a structure.

You have already seen that *structure* is a general term including many particulars, a bridge being one of them. The second step, then, is to differentiate *bridge* from all other structures—buildings, houses, towers, and so forth. This can be done by naming its function:

> A bridge is a structure *carrying a roadway over a depression or obstacle.*

Examine these definitions by classification:

WORD	FAMILY	DIFFERENTIATION
Bird	vertebrate	covered with feathers and having wings.
Insect	invertebrate	having head, thorax, and abdomen, three pairs of legs and one or two pair of wings.
Chair	seat	having four legs and a back, for one person.
House	building	serving as living quarters for one or more families.

In defining by classification, there are three missteps to guard against.

1. Look at this definition of *net* from Samuel Johnson's dictionary:

> A net is any reticulated fabric, decussated at regular intervals, with interstices at the intersections.

Since you know what a net is, you can probably make out what this definition says. But suppose you do not know what a net is. Could you possibly make sense from this definition without looking up several words in the dictionary? Probably not. So when you see the necessity of defining a word, follow this rule:

> Do not use words that might not be clear to the reader (that is, obscure, ambiguous, or figurative).

Suppose you read this definition: *A democracy is a government in which the citizens are sovereign.* This is a perfectly good definition as long as you know what the word *sovereign* means. The writer could have avoided the use of this word by spelling out its meaning. For instance, he might have written this clearer definition: *A democracy is a government in which the citizens hold supreme power by periodically electing, either directly or indirectly, their representation in the government.*

2. Consider this definition: *A democracy has a democratic form of government.* Here no defining has taken place, because the definition offered leaves the reader at the same place he started. The writer has used a form of the defined word in the definition itself. This definition has the same trouble: *A good man is one who performs good deeds.* The word that is being defined here is *good,* but this word has also been used in the definition of it, so nothing has been clearly defined. Stick to this rule, also:

> Do not use any form of the defined word in the definition of the word.

3. Look at this definition: *Democracy is when the citizens are sovereign.* You have probably been told throughout your scholastic career that you cannot define by saying that something "is when. . . ." Logically, you cannot make the adverbial construction (showing condition), *when the citizens are sovereign,* equal to the noun, *democracy;* but the use of the verb *is* says that they are. In defining, then, you must also remember this rule:

> The word defined must always be equal to the definition.

That is, wherever the defined word is used, you should be able to substitute your definition in its place. You can say, for instance, *The government of the United States is a democracy,* but when you try to substitute for the word the definition of democracy just considered, complete nonsense results: *The government of the United States is when the citizens are sovereign.* So a good definition of democracy is needed, one that can be substituted wherever the word itself is used. Here is a definition that will work: *Democracy is a form of government in which the citizens are sovereign.* Now we can substitute this definition for the word *democracy* in the sentence, *The government of the United States is a democracy: The government of the United States is a form of government in which the citizens are sovereign.* Note that placing the word in its family and then applying differentiation corrects this misstep.

Definition by Synonym

One of the easiest ways to define is by using other words that mean the same thing as the defined word but that are likely to be more easily understood. For instance, if you are not certain your reader will know what *prevaricating* means, you can define it by saying that it means *lying* or *fibbing.* Or you can say that to *limit* is to *restrict* or to *define.* Or you might define *bad* as meaning *bath* in German, but as meaning *evil, wicked,* or *naughty* in English. In defining by the use of synonym, you must understand two points.

1. Synonyms are useful in definition only when they are closer to the reader's experience than is the word defined.

2. Usually synonyms are not definitions but only approximations. They may best be used to clarify other kinds of definitions.

Definition by example or illustration

Sometimes it is possible to make clear a word unknown to the reader by pointing out an example of something that is known and that is the same thing. For instance, you can define the color green by pointing to a plot of live grass and saying, "Green is the color of that grass." Or if you happen to have anything at hand of the color you want to define, you can simply hold it out and say, "Magenta is this color." Or if you do not have any of the color at hand you can say, "Magenta is red with some blue in it—a purplish red." To define by illustration you can give a brief narrative (a story) that explains what is being defined. Here is an example of how you might define *spoiled child.*

> When Roger is asked to do something he doesn't want to do, he sticks out his tongue or simply turns away with no response at all. He demands what he wants and gets it, or else he lies on the floor and screams until it is forthcoming.

Definition by Enumeration

In defining words that are the names of general classes of objects, you can sometimes define the word by simply listing the members of the class represented by that word. For example, you can define *decathlon* by listing the athletic events included.

> The decathlon is an athletic event in which each contestant competes in the 100-meter, 400-meter, and 1500-meter runs, the 110-meter high hurdles, the javelin and discus throws, shot put, pole vault, high jump, and broad jump.

Or you can define the Pentateuch by listing the books of the Bible that compose it.

> The Pentateuch is Genesis, Exodus, Leviticus, Numbers, and Deuteronomy.

Some classes are too large to enumerate, but most frequently you can list enough of the members of the class so that the definition is made understandable. For instance, to list all the seasonings would take up more space than the definition is worth and would make tedious reading. But some of the seasonings can be listed and the effect is the same as if they were all listed.

> Salt, pepper, thyme, oregano, marjoram, are common seasonings.
> Citrus fruits are such fruits as lemons, oranges and grapefruit.

Note that the definition admits the listing is not complete. And, again, you must be sure that the reader will be more familiar with the members of the class than with the name of the class itself.

Definition by Function (Operational Definition)

Frequently you can define by describing how an object functions or operates. Definition by function is particularly useful in defining the name of a machine or mechanism, because showing what a machine does will usually serve as sufficient definition. The functional definition is not limited to defining the names of objects, however. For instance, you might define *prejudice* by using the functional method. A dictionary definition of prejudice might appear in some such form as this: *A preconceived, especially unfavorable, judgment or opinion.* A functional definition would show how prejudice operates.

> A prejudice is a judgment or opinion about a person, race, religion, nation, or any particular group or object without careful consideration of facts. To feel antagonism at first meeting toward a student from a rival college without actually knowing the student is to be prejudiced toward him.

Or, *claustrophobia* might be defined in a dictionary as *morbid fear of enclosed or confined places.* A definition by function, which might be added to this definition by way of further explanation, would come out in this way:

> Persons who, when confined in a small, enclosed space such as an elevator, exhibit a rapid quickening of heart beat, acute agitation, and a desperate desire to leave the enclosed space are suffering from a mental disturbance known as claustrophobia.

EXERCISES

A. If any of these statements is not acceptable as definitions, indicate specifically what is wrong with it. If any is acceptable, mark it *C.*
  1. Lapidation is when you hurl stones at someone.
  2. A lanyard is a rope used in firing certain types of cannon.
  3. A proletarian is a member of the proletariat.
  4. Syneresis is closely associated with dieresis and synizesis because all of them concern the coalescence of two vowels or syllables.
  5. English is where expository writing is learned.
  6. Gamosepalous is the same as synsepalous.
  7. Tabasco is the trade name of a sauce made from red pepper.
  8. Tetrameter is a line of verse consisting of four metrical feet.
  9. Second childhood means senility or dotage.
  10. Debate is an element basic to any democracy.

B. Write your own definitions of the following words, using two methods of defining for each. Do not consult your dictionary.

1.	Book	5.	Lamp
2.	Box	6.	Money
3.	Free enterprise	7.	Morals
4.	Friend	8.	Vehicle

The Extended Definition

Now that you have learned the methods of defining, you are ready to write an extended definition. An extended definition is ordinarily a paragraph, but it can be much longer, using a combination of definition methods to explain explicitly the defined word, and starting with a definition by classification. A diagram of the paragraph developed by an extended definition will help clarify.

DEFINITION BY CLASSIFICATION

Clarification (usually of differentia) by any pertinent means: illustration, examples, contrast, comparison, detail, synonyms, enumeration, function.

To further clarify, here are some students' extended definitions.

Jargon is a special vocabulary understandable only to the users. In Elmstown, one has only to pay a visit to Joe's Wagon Diner, at Tenth and Canal, to hear examples of its use. Table orders are taken by the waiters and given to the kitchen in such a manner that one hears expressions like, "One-eyed jacks up, no hog," meaning an order of two eggs fried on one side and no bacon; or "One brown with dogs, add straight," meaning an order of hash brown potatoes with sausage, and coffee without cream or sugar; or "Cream it with hens," meaning creamed eggs on toast; or "Dunk one all the way," meaning doughnut and coffee with cream and sugar.

This paragraph starts with a definition by classification and then extends the definition by adding a series of short examples to explain what jargon is. Here are three more example paragraphs of extended definitions.

A "turista" is any human being who finds himself in strange surroundings that he is not able to appreciate. The word is usually employed to describe middle-aged persons who have just started traveling. It is a fit description for a woman who upon arriving at the Grand Canyon, rushes to the gift shop to buy postcards before she has had a look at the sight she has traveled to see. The word, although it has a feminine ending, is applied to the male traveler who goes to the Louvre and stares at female forms in the flesh and not at the Venus de Milo. The "turista" is constantly comparing his present surroundings with the heaven-on-earth where he lives, making all listeners wonder why he had not remained in that choice place. He is a steak-and-potato man and is constantly griping about the food. He refuses to eat reindeer meat in Norway, but longs for it as he is eating lasagna in Italy, proving to the uninterested listeners that he has been to Norway. The word is never applied to anyone except Americans, meaning anyone from the United States, and is used by persons in foreign countries to show their dislike for individuals who spend their money ostentatiously while traveling.

Elephant jokes, popular some time ago, are humorous devices consisting of two lines—a question and an answer—in which an elephant is pointlessly involved. An example of this joke would be, "What was the elephant doing on the expressway?" and the answer, "About three miles an hour." Or, with a side flavor, "What do you call the black stuff between an elephant's toes?" Answer, "Slow natives." Or, with a risque twist, "How do you make an elephant fly?" Answer, "First, you get an eight-foot zipper." Often these jokes are presented in a series, each joke related to the last. A short example would be, "How do you tell an elephant from a bluebird?" Answer, "Elephants live in trees." Question, "How did the elephant get flat feet?" Answer, "From jumping out of trees." Question, "Why do elephants jump out of trees?" Answer, "How else could they get down?"

A thunderstorm is a weather disturbance having lightning and, consequently, thunder within it. There need not be rain falling, but without lightning it is merely a rain shower and not a thunderstorm. Thundershowers come in three types—air mass thunderstorms, frontal thunderstorms, and thunderstorms caused by unstable air over mountains. Air mass thunderstorms are common along the Gulf Coast in the afternoon during the summer. Frontal thunderstorms occur in the fall, winter, and spring along and ahead of cold fronts. Since there are no mountains in this area, the third type of thunderstorm never occurs here. Sometimes towering to heights of 50,000 or 60,000 feet, thunderstorms can be quite severe, bringing rain and hail and sometimes spawning tornadoes.

EXERCISES

Select three of these topics and write a paragraph of extended definition for each.

Beauty of soul	Adequate diet
Courtesy in everyday affairs	Vivacity of youth
"Decency" at the beach	The home remedy
Ethical behavior	Jokes
Worthwhile fishing trips	Slang
Any new slang word	Freedom of speech
Well-dressed coeds	Political conservatives

Sportsmanship   Practical jokes
The joys of Christmas   Excellent teachers
                             Social fraternities

PARAGRAPH DEVELOPMENT
BY USE OF ILLUSTRATION

Illustration, as used to support a topic sentence in the developmental paragraph, is narrative, that is, it tells a story. It usually gives a chronological account of what happened in a certain situation that would give validity to the topic sentence. Illustrations can be either real or hypothetical. You can use an account of some event you actually know about, or you can, in effect, "make up" one, provided the reader understands that the illustration is hypothetical. Usually the hypothetical illustration starts with something like "Suppose such-and-such a thing happened. What would be the result?" Then the writer goes on to supply a narrative of what would happen in the hypothetical situation.

Paragraphs may be developed by two kinds of illustrations—short and extended. A collection of short illustrations, all supporting the topic sentence, may be used as a paragraph. Usually, the narrative in a short illustration is quite brief. Or an extended illustration, a single, relatively long narrative, may constitute the paragraph. Of course, any combination of extended and short illustrations may be used to support the topic sentence.

The paragraph developed by the use of illustration appears as in this diagram.

TOPIC SENTENCE

A narrative or a number of narratives, in any combination, that specifically illustrates the validity of the topic sentence.

Now, look at some examples of students' paragraphs using illustration. The first paragraph uses a series of short illustrations in support of the topic sentence.

American history is a record of man's courage. During the Revolution, Paul Revere, a Boston silversmith, rode his horse through the night to warn the Massachusetts colonists that the British were coming. Daniel Boone, Kentucky trailblazer and Indian fighter; Davy Crockett, hero of the Battle of the Alamo; and Lewis and Clark, leaders of the trail expedition to Oregon, all did their share in shaping the growth of a young country struggling against unknown obstacles. In more recent times, Charles Lindbergh, who by making the first nonstop flight from New York to Paris, established the importance of air power to our country; General Douglas MacArthur, victorious against the Japanese after early defeat; and John F. Kennedy, who nearly lost his life as a PT boat commander in World War II but lived to become President of the United States, all displayed the personal bravery so apparent in American history.

This paragraph uses seven short illustrations, arranged chronologically in American history, to support its topic sentence. The next paragraph is an example of the extended illustration.

Poor communication between the administration and staff results in misunderstandings among the employees of the Chemist's Laboratory. Recently, for instance, the department head told a graduate student employee, a good worker who had been carefully trained by another administrator in the same department, to go home and change out of Bermuda shorts or to consider himself fired. The incident, which occurred while several women employees were present, embarrassed the student so deeply that he determined not to work for such a man. The student resigned, and the department lost a well-trained and efficient worker because neither administrator had taken the responsibility of telling the employee what dress was acceptable for work.

Here is another example of the use of a series of short illustrations.

Many people in show business have become famous because of a "gimmick." In the thirties, for example, such entertainers as Helen Kane with her "boo-boop-a-doop," and Joe Penner with "Wanna buy a duck?" rose to national prominence. In the fifties, Elvis Presley achieved adulation and stardom as a rock-and-roll singer by wiggling his hips and charming the teenage world by his wild gyrations. Frank Fontaine became popular because of a humorously stupid laugh. And more recently, the Beatles, an English singing group, were an immediate sensation, not so much for their singing as primarily for their clothes and long hair.

Here is another use of extended illustration, a hypothetical one.

Despite the general opinion that it is recreation, an all night fishing excursion is more work than pleasure. Suppose, for example, a typical fisherman decides to fish in his favorite lake, an afternoon's drive from his home. Since he plans to spend the night, he will spend all morning packing his gear—boat, fish lines, bait, food, cooking utensils, tent, bedding, and clothing. Then, after driving all afternoon to reach the lake, he will begin the tiring job of establishing camp. This task completed, he must back his boat trailer to the edge of the lake and laboriously ease his boat into the water. He then must find what he considers the perfect spot for setting out and baiting his lines. On his return to camp, he will perspire over an open fire while preparing his supper. After supper and again at two o'clock in the morning, he must run his lines, rebaiting where necessary. If he is lucky, he may net a fish or two before returning to camp for a few minutes of rest. As the sun appears on the horizon, he will cook and eat breakfast and begin to repack his gear for the long journey home. Four hours later, after an exhausting drive, he will walk into the house and collapse on the bed for a well-earned rest.

You will note that this paragraph does not contain an actual illustration, that is, the experience recounted in the paragraph did not happen to a specific person, necessarily, but it simply indicates what would likely happen to anyone on an overnight fishing trip.

The next sample is similar to the preceding one in that it involves a hypothetical individual and situation. But this example was written by a respected, published writer.

The tribes we have described have all of them their non-participating "abnormal" individuals. The individual in Dobu who was thoroughly disoriented was the man who was naturally friendly and found activity an end in itself. He was a pleasant fellow who did not seek to overthrow his fellows or to punish them. He worked for anyone who asked him, and he was not filled by a terror of the dark like his fellows, and he did not, as they did, utterly inhibit simple public responses of friendliness toward women closely related, like a wife or sister. He often patted them playfully in public. In any other Dobuan this was scandalous behavior, but in him it was regarded as merely silly. The village treated him in a kindly enough fashion, not taking advantage of him or making a sport of ridiculing him, but he was definitely regarded as one who was outside the game.[5]

The next two paragraphs from the same book indicate how the author uses an extended illustration about a real individual as he has been observed in the Zuni society. Note that the illustration extends over two paragraphs but that each paragraph makes its own point with its own topic sentence.

The dilemma of such an individual is often most successfully solved by doing violence to his strongest natural impulses and accepting the role the culture honors. In case he is a person to whom social recognition is necessary, it is ordinarily his only possible course. One of the most striking individuals in Zuni had accepted this necessity. In a society that thoroughly distrusts authority of any sort, he had a native personal magnetism that singled him out in any group. In a society that exalts moderation and the easiest way, he was turbulent and could act violently upon occasion. In a society that praises a pliant personality that "talks lots"—that is, that chatters in a friendly fashion—he was scornful and aloof. Zuni's only reaction to such personalities is to brand them as witches. He was said to have been seen peering through a window from outside, and this is a sure mark of a witch. At any rate, he got drunk one day and boasted that they could not kill him. He was taken before the war priest who hung him by his thumbs from the rafters till he should confess to his witchcraft. This is the usual procedure in a charge of witchcraft. However, he dispatched a messenger to the government troops. When they came, his shoulders were already crippled for life, and the officer of the law was left with no recourse but to imprison the war priests who had been responsible for the enormity. One of these war priests was probably the most respected and important person in recent Zuni history, and when he returned after imprisonment in the state penitentiary he never resumed his priestly offices. He regarded his power as broken. It was a revenge that is probably unique in Zuni history. It involved, of course, a challenge to the priesthoods, against whom the witch by his act openly aligned himself.

The course of his life in the forty years that followed this defiance was not, however, what we might easily predict. A witch is not barred from his membership in cult groups because he has been condemned, and the way to recognition lay through such activity. He possessed a remarkable verbal memory and a sweet singing voice. He learned unbelievable stories of mythology, of esoteric ritual, of

[5]Ruth Benedict, *Patterns of Culture.* Copyright 1934 by Ruth Benedict. Reprinted by permission of Houghton Mifflin Company.

cult songs. Many hundrds of pages of stories and ritual poetry were taken down from his dictation before he died, and he regarded his songs as much more extensive. He became indispensable in ceremonial life and before he died was the governor of Zuni. The congenial bent of his personality threw him into irreconcilable conflict with his society, and he solved his dilemma by turning an incidental talent to account. As we might well expect, he was not a happy man. As governor of Zuni, and high in his cult groups, a marked man in his community, he was obsessed by death. He was a cheated man in the midst of a mildly happy populace.[6]

EXERCISES

A. Select two of these topic sentences and write two separate paragraphs. In one, use a series of short illustrations to support the topic sentence. In the other, use an extended illustration.
  1. Our senior class represented a cross section of society.
  2. The major did not always act so wisely.
  3. The clean-up drive produced noteworthy results.
  4. Students are uncomfortable in the new elementary school.
  5. Cheating is (is not) widespread in .... High School.
  6. Stylish dress is outlandish.
B. This exercise reviews some of the material already covered.
  1. Look again at the paragraph about American history on page 92, and answer the following questions.
    a. What is the pointer in the topic sentence?
    b. Are there any sentences that do not help to establish this pointer as valid?
    c. What is the purpose of the phrases *During the Revolution* and *In more recent times*?
    d. What is there in the last sentence that ties it to the first sentence?
    e. Would you say, then, that this paragraph is coherent? Why or why not?
  2. Answer these questions on the paragraph about fishing on page 93.
    a. What is the pointer in the topic sentence?
    b. Examine the subjects of the sentences. Is a consistent point of view maintained?
    c. In what other ways is coherence achieved?
    d. About two-thirds of the way through the paragraph the word *perspire* is used. Would you prefer another word here? Why or why not?

[6]*Ibid.*

3. These questions concern the two paragraphs about the Zuni society on page 94.

   a. What is the pointer in the topic sentence of the first paragraph? Of the second paragraph?   ·

   b. In the first paragraph, what coherence device is employed in the sentence that starts *In a society that thoroughly distrusts. . . .* and in the next few sentences?

   c. What is the purpose of the phrase *At any rate*, about half-way through the first paragraph? Has the principle of unity been violated just before the use of this phrase?

   d. Look at this sentence a little more than halfway through the first paragraph: *This is the usual procedure in a charge of witchcraft.* As you read through the paragraph (try it aloud), this sentence seems to be out of the tone of the rest of the paragraph. What makes it seem so? Try to rewrite it to make it fit in better. You might try including it in the preceding sentence.

   e. What is the purpose of *however* in the first sentence of the second paragraph?

   f. What purpose is served by *As we might well expect*, in the third sentence from the end of the second paragraph?

   g. Is the second paragraph coherent? What means of achieving coherence are used?

PARAGRAPH DEVELOPMENT
BY COMPARISON OR CONTRAST

Comparison and contrast, as developmental methods, are so much alike that they can be considered together. First, the two terms must be defined.

COMPARISON: indicates similarities between two objects, people, places, or ideas for the purpose of clarifying or explaining one or the other.

CONTRAST: indicates differences between two objects, people, places, or ideas for the purpose of clarifying or explaining one or the other.

Comparison shows similarities, and contrast shows difference. Developing a paragraph by comparison or by contrast is not difficult, but it is better to compare or contrast point-by-point than to take the whole of the first object of comparison and then the whole of the other object. For instance, if you were comparing two cars it would be better to compare, say, the performance of one to the performance of the other, next their economy, and finally their appearance, than to describe these three points for one car and then describe them for* the other.

Here is a diagram of the paragraph developed by comparison or contrast.

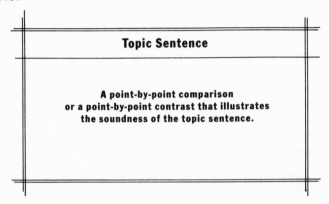

Topic Sentence

A point-by-point comparison or a point-by-point contrast that illustrates the soundness of the topic sentence.

Note how the following student paragraph makes this point-by-point comparison between a school and a game of basketball.

School is like a game of basketball. In both, the time is short, and the student uses all his resources in the class as the player does in the game. The student has a background of knowledge that enables him to meet the challenges in class; the player relies on ability he has acquired previously. The student begins on registration day a period in which he matches wits with his opponent, the professor. The first whistle of the basketball game starts the player matching his wits with the opposing team. The student relaxes over the weekends, taking this time to catch his breath; time out in the baskeball game allows the player to catch his breath. The student can slow down the class, if he is tired, by turning it into a bull session. The basketball player can also slow the game. Each is aware that he runs the risk of being punished, as the professor can give a pop quiz, or the referee can call a foul. Each participant is striving for a measure of his ability, a grade for the student and a score for the player. At the end of the term, the student looks anxiously at the bulletin board just outside the classroom for the final verdict. The player's eyes scan the scoreboard for the outcome of his efforts. The result is the same. If the student makes a good grade or the player has the high score, both are pleased with their efforts. If either loses—but that is too horrible to think about.

And here is a paragraph written by a student, a young lady who was very fond of her new foreign car. She planned her paragraph around the same point-by-point comparison.

> The proud owners of big American automobiles look with scorn at my little foreign car and with contempt call it a beetle. Well, I suppose it is almost a beetle. Nature carefully designed oval-shaped, low bodies for beetles to decrease air resistance, and my tiny horse-less carriage is as smooth, oval, and low as any real beetle. Most beetles are actually poor flyers and indeed some, like my car, never fly. A true member of the beetle family is powerful but slow; my small auto cannot go over sixty miles per hour, but it can climb steep curving roads well in spite of ice, rain, or standing water. Bugs take in energy-giving food anteriorly, and my bug-car has its gasoline tank near its nose also. Real beetles have posterior air intake tubes just like my little foreign car, although the real beetles have more of them. Normally I dislike bugs, but I am so fond of my beetle-like Volkswagen that I may grow to like all beetles.

This paragraph compares first the appearance of the two objects, next the performance of the two, and finally the position of fuel and air intake openings.

This next paragraph is developed by use of contrast. Note that again the point-by-point plan is used, but here in contrasting rather than in comparing.

> The modern kitchen is different from the old-style type. It even looks different. The charm of the old kitchen lay in its design, from the wallpaper to the curtains to the tablecloth; but the modern kitchen has no designs, only shiny chrome and brilliant color. There's a different atmosphere, too. Grandma's kitchen was a place to talk things over, to have a hot drink and relax while savoring the odors of bread baking in the oven, to leisurely plan and put loving thought into every meal prepared there. But the modern kitchen is con-structed for speed, for the fastest and easiest way to get the food on the table and the dishes washed so that the cook can go on to other activities. The modern kitchen seems to have a different role to play in our lives. Instead of being a center of family life, it has become a laundry, dining room, and office for the increasingly complicated job of the homemaker.

This paragraph compares the old and the new kitchen on three points: their appearance, their atmosphere, and their roles in family life.

The next paragraph, a comparison, was written by a disgruntled married student.

Special words have been used to sympathize with the "golfer's widow," but no terms directly apply to the amateur mechanic's wife, who is no better off. Both are often left stranded for hours with no cars while the laundry waits to be washed and the pantry to be filled. The golfer cannot stand the thought of his friends putting on the green without him, and the auto maniac insists on being present after each exciting mechanical failure. Either situation may leave the wife floundering in a welter of broken social engagements. Although it is worse in some ways to break appointments for lack of transportation or an escort, the mechanic's wife and the golfer's wife are placed at further social disadvantage by knowing that, come spring, when afternoon picnics and cook-outs are enticing, they dare not plan them. After a winter of being cooped up in the house, the amateur mechanic wants to polish his car as well as those of his buddies, and the golfer wants to join his cronies on the golf course. Both leave their wives to wonder how the myth of "family companionship" persists.

EXERCISE

Select two of these topic sentences. Write one paragraph using comparison as a means of development and another paragraph using contrast.

1. The P.E. teacher insisted that the class would benefit far more if they chose swimming rather than fencing (archery, golf, badminton, field hockey, handball) for the second semester's work.
2. My sister inherited her physical characteristics from our mother.
3. The prospective buyer has little choice among today's cars.
4. It was a tossup between the petite, dark-eyed vixen and the stately blonde from Sioux City.
5. Mrs. Smith said that one conversation piece in the living room was enough.
6. Home cooking is not what it used to be.
7. Youth has "rebelled" before.
8. My mother and father illustrate the axiom that opposites attract.
9. I have not found college so different from high school (or the opposite).
10. The feud between Mrs. Suffle and her neighbor included even the landscaping of their lawns.

PARAGRAPH DEVELOPMENT BY REASONS

The use of reasons in paragraph development has already been discussed in the section about maintaining unity in the paragraph. Recall that example paragraphs in the section gave two or more reasons for the validity of the topic sentence and then supported those reasons. Also recall that this pattern of development is the one suggested in the first chapter for the whole paper, except that in the paper the reasons (topic sentences) support the thesis statement of the paper. Therefore, because a paragraph is a small paper, the same method of development can be used in the paragraph.

In one of the exercises of an earlier chapter, you were asked to analyze a paragraph by E. B. White. This paragraph was developed by using reasons. Have another look at it.

> It is a miracle that New York works at all. *The whole thing is implausible.* Every time the residents brush their teeth, millions of gallons of water must be drawn from the Catskills and the hills of Westchester. When a young man in Manhattan writes a letter to his girl in Brooklyn, the love message gets blown to her through a pneumatic tube—*pfft*—just like that. The subterranean system of telephone cables, power lines, steam pipes, gas mains and sewer pipes is reason enough to abandon the island to the gods and the weevils. Every time an incision is made in the pavement, the noisy surgeons expose ganglia that are tangled beyond belief. By rights *New York should have destroyed itself long ago,* from panic or fire or rioting or failure of some vital supply line in its circulatory system or from deep labyrinthine short circuit. Long ago the city should have experienced an insoluble traffic snarl at some impossible bottleneck. It should have perished of hunger when food lines failed for a few days. It should have been wiped out by a plague starting in its slums or carried in by ships' rats. It should have been overwhelmed by the sea that licks at it on every side. The workers in its myriad cells should have succumbed to nerves, from the fearful pall of smoke-fog that drifts over every few days from Jersey, blotting out all light at noon, and leaving the high offices suspended, men groping and depressed, and the sense of world's end. It should have been touched in the head by the August heat and gone off its rocker.[7]

The topic sentence of this paragraph is the first sentence. Its pointer is *miracle*. The two reasons that support this topic sentence are italicized in the paragraph. In its simplest outline form, the paragraph appears like this:

Topic Sentence: It is a miracle that New York works at all.
Main Reason 1: The whole thing is implausible.
Main Reason 2: New York should have destroyed itself long ago.

[7]E. B. White, *Here Is New York,* pp. 24–25. Copyright 1949 by E. B. White. Used by permission of Harper & Row, Publishers, Inc.

This outline as it stands could be assembled into a paragraph.

> It is a miracle that New York works at all. The whole thing is implausible for a number of reasons. There is so much congestion that New York should have destroyed itself long ago.

But you have learned that this is not a good paragraph because it does not supply details as supporting reasons. White did it like this:

Topic Sentence: It is a miracle that New York works at all.
  Main Reason 1: The whole thing is implausible.
    Supporting Reason 1: Water must come from a distance.
    Supporting Reason 2: Mail is carried through tubes.
    Supporting Reason 3: Subterranean lines, cables, and pipes are hopelessly tangled.
  Main Reason 2: New York should have destroyed itself,
    Supporting Reason 1: From insoluble traffic snarls.
    Supporting Reason 2: From hunger through failure of food lines.
    Supporting Reason 3: From plague through slums or rats.
    Supporting Reason 4: From the sea.
    Supporting Reason 5: From workers' nerves.
    Supporting Reason 6: From insanity.

A paragraph from the section on comparison and contrast may also be used to illustrate paragraph development through reasons. Look at it again.

> The modern kitchen is different from the old-style type. *It even looks different.* The charm of the old kitchen lay in its design, from the wallpaper to the curtains to the tablecloth; but the modern kitchen has no designs, only shiny chrome and brilliant color. *There's a different atmosphere,* too. Grandma's kitchen was a place to talk things over, to have a hot drink and relax while savoring the odor of bread baking in the oven, to leisurely plan and put loving thought into every meal prepared there. But the modern kitchen is constructed for speed, for the fastest and easiest way to get the food on the table and the dishes washed so that the cook can go on to other activities. *The modern kitchen seems to have a different role to play in our lives.* Instead of being a center of family life, it has become a laundry, dining room, and office for the increasingly complicated job of the homemaker.

The topic sentence is the first sentence in the paragraph. The pointer is *different.* The paragraph lists three reasons for the difference. In diagram form, the paragraph looks like this:

Topic Sentence: The modern kitchen is different from the old-style type.
   Reason 1: It has a different appearance.
   Reason 2: It has a different atmosphere.
   Reason 3: It plays a different role in family life.

The development of each of the three reasons is accomplished by the use of contrast, that is, contrasting the old kitchen to the new on each of these three points. The paragraph, then, is developed by two methods—reasons and contrast.

EXERCISES

A. Using two of these topic sentences, write two outlines for paragraphs to be developed by reason. You may take the opposite point of view of any of these topic sentences.
  1. We lost the game because of our star player's mistakes.
  2. Dormitory life teaches the freshman self-reliance.
  3. Sally did not want to have a date with him.
  4. Dress helps to make the man.
  5. Her teaching methods were directed toward making the student think.
  6. Downtown business centers in cities are certain to decrease in importance.
  7. A universal metric system would allow freer world trade.
  8. (Your school) was the proper choice for me.
  9. Charlie decided not to attend the tea.
  10. A car is necessary at school.

Follow this outline form:

Topic Sentence:
  Main Reason 1:
    Supporting Reason 1:
    Supporting Reason 2:
  Main Reason 2:
    Supporting Reason 1:
    Supporting Reason 2:
  Main Reason 3:
    Supporting Reason 1:
    Supporting Reason 2:

Your outlines must have at least two main reasons plus as many as you may need to develop the paragraph adequately. Each main reason must also have at least two supporting reasons.

B. Write paragraphs from the two outlines composed for Exercise A.

METHODS OF DEVELOPMENT IN COMBINATION

Ordinarily, paragraphs are not developed solely by one of these methods you have just studied but by any combination of methods. The methods selected are those that seem to the writer the most suitable to explain and establish the topic sentence. Nor, ordinarily, does the experienced writer deliberately determine to develop a paragraph by any specific method. He unconsciously selects methods as he writes; nevertheless, he does use methods. For example, here are some paragraphs written by experienced writers. Note how they combine methods in a single paragraph.

1 Lasers—there are several varieties—are rather surprisingly
2 simple devices which generate highly disciplined and coherent
3 light rays. To appreciate their impact one must first realize
4 that until a few years ago an important dividing line cut across
5 the electromagnetic frequency spectrum just above the upper
6 limits of the microwave region. Below this divide there were
7 transistors and electron tubes which could generate the coherent
8 signals necessary for communications or computers or any of
9 the other tasks of modern electronics. Above it, in the infrared
10 and optical regions, there were only incoherent thermal sources
11 —the sun, light bulbs, arc lamps, flames. The electromagnetic
12 radiation from these sources is highly undisciplined, containing
13 waves traveling in all possible directions and made up of a
14 scrambled mixture of all possible frequencies.
15 The development of the laser as a coherent light source
16 means that this division is now gone. Note that most lasers
17 emit considerably less total power than, say, a hundred-watt
18 bulb. But the light bulb, which is incoherent, emits its energy
19 into so many frequencies and directions that the amount emit-
20 ted into any single specific frequency and direction is minute.
21 By contrast, the laser, which is coherent, emits all of its energy
22 at a single frequency and in a single direction and in some
23 cases does so in a single brief but extremely intense burst.
24 Within its single frequency and direction, therefore, the laser
25 is incomparably brighter than, say, the sun or any other thermal
26 light source.[8]

These two paragraphs are definition paragraphs. They attempt to define lasers in nonscientific terms that an ordinary reader can

[8]Anthony E. Siegman, "The Laser: Astounding Beam of Light," *Stanford Today*, Autumn, 1964. Reprinted by permission of *Stanford Today*, Leland Stanford Junior University.

understand, and several methods of development are used in the definition. Note that the first sentence is a simple definition by classification. From lines two through nine, the author uses explanation of background reinforced by reason. In line ten, he defines *incoherent thermal sources* by enumeration. The last part of line eleven starts a definition by classification of the word *undisciplined* as applied to electromagnetic radiation. Lines fifteen through twenty-four offer contrast as a method of development. Note that *incoherent* and *coherent light sources* are defined in this contrast. The last sentence is a conclusion, as shown by the transition word *therefore*.

Here is another paragraph by an experienced writer.

[1]An Indian coffeehouse, like an Indian bazaar, has its own peculiar atmosphere. [2]It is a cheerful, unpretentious place in which to dawdle, encounter friends, talk, discuss, gossip. [3]Students make fiery speeches to each other; women meet for a break in the morning's shopping; idlers stop by for a rest, to watch the world go by, to pick up a chance colleague. [4]The actual drinking of coffee is the least important part of the whole affair. [5]Looking around at the tables, I couldn't help thinking that this particular sort of place doesn't exist in Moscow. [6]There, one can find restaurants (mostly rather expensive by any standard), or "Parks of Culture and Rest," or hotel dining rooms, and several varieties of bar ranging from the *pivnaya*, where as a rule you can't even sit down, where women are seldom seen, and where the customers walk to the bar, order a drink, down it and leave, all within the space of five minutes, to the *stolovoye*, which is considered more refined, more suitable for women, and where ordinary vodka is not served, though wines and brandy are brought to your table. [7]But India is not a drinking country—even in the states where there is no prohibition. [8]The sight of drunks being thrown out of restaurants with the offhand ruthlessness that Russians employ for such occasions is extremely rare in India.[9]

In this paragraph, sentences two, three, and four use detail to explain the atmosphere of the Indian coffeehouse. Sentences five, six, seven, and eight are concerned with a contrast between the drinking habits of Indians and of Russians. Note that sentence six is filled with detail to describe the Russian bars.

[9]Santha Ramu Rau, "Return to India," *The Reporter*, June, 1960. Published by The Reporter Magazine Company. Copyright © 1960 by *The Reporter*. Reprinted by permission of William Morris Agency, Inc.

Putting the Parts Together:
The Whole Paper

5
Now that you have studied the parts of the five-hundred-word paper, it is time to put all the parts together into a paper. First, as a reminder, look again at the five-hundred-word paper in a diagram, presented this time in a slightly different version because of your knowledge of it.

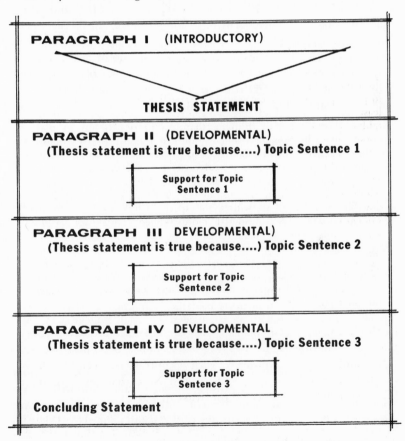

PARAGRAPH I (INTRODUCTORY)

THESIS STATEMENT

PARAGRAPH II (DEVELOPMENTAL)
(Thesis statement is true because....) Topic Sentence 1

Support for Topic
Sentence 1

PARAGRAPH III DEVELOPMENTAL)
(Thesis statement is true because....) Topic Sentence 2

Support for Topic
Sentence 2

PARAGRAPH IV DEVELOPMENTAL
(Thesis statement is true because....) Topic Sentence 3

Support for Topic
Sentence 3

Concluding Statement

This, again, is the pattern you will use in writing your papers. You are now ready to write one, but before you do, have a clear understanding of what your instructor will look for when he marks your paper. The grade your instructor assigns your paper will be a composite assessment of how well you do on three points:

1. *Content*—Your instructor will decide whether you have a meaningful subject and whether your development of it has been full and logical.

2. *Organization*—He will determine whether you have an acceptable thesis statement supported by topic sentences that are in turn supported by evidence presented in the paragraphs.

3. *Mechanics*—He will mark unacceptable spelling and punctuation, poor sentence structure (for instance, incomplete sentences), disunity and lack of coherence, and poor diction (that is, word choice, including listless verbs and overuse of adverbs).

Bear in mind that a real weakness on any *one* of these points will influence the grader. You can, for example, show good content and organization, but if the mechanics of your paper are poor, your grade could be disappointing. Similarly, your mechanics can be perfect and your organization good, but if your paper lacks ideas of consequence or is dull, the result may be the same. You will need to find an acceptable balance among these three points.

To further understand what your instructor will be looking for, consider the next four students' papers, which are analyzed as an instructor might do it. Examine them one paragraph at a time.

THE STUDENT AND CLASSIC COMICS

High school students, usually not avid readers of comic books, often resort to substituting classic comics for required reading books. Basically honest, many of these students, under pressure of heavy assignments and extracurricular activities, think of the classic comic merely as a short cut to an assignment. Although students may be able to write a plot summary, they are cheating themselves when they take the easy way out.

This paragraph fulfills the requirements for a short introductory paragraph. It starts with a general statement and ends with a specific thesis statement: Students cheat themselves when they take the easy way out (by substituting classic comics for required reading). The remainder of the paper must show why students cheat themselves through this procedure. Look at the first developmental paragraph.

> The student who depends on the comic book version of the world's great literature often deprives himself of an accurate presentation of the original story. For example, if he reads the comic version of Twain's *A Connecticut Yankee*, which eliminates any attempt at satire, he receives the impression that Twain was making an early effort at some type of science fiction. A student who relies on the comic classic of *Huckleberry Finn* misses many of Huck's adventures, such as the Grangerford episode, and finds the story ending in a manner that would startle the author. The unfortunate student who makes his book report from the comic classic *The House of Seven Gables* will overemphasize the Pyncheon ancestors and the family curse, saying little about Hepzibah, Clifford, and the other characters because mysterious deaths and family curses create better mystery stories than the effect of these circumstances on characters.

This developmental paragraph has a proper topic sentence, as the first sentence in the paragraph, indicating one reason that the thesis statement is valid: The student does not get an accurate presentation of the original story. To give support for this topic sentence, three short illustrations are used from three famous works of fiction to show how each story is twisted in its comic book version. Because the pointer in the topic sentence is *deprived* and each illustration indicates how this deprivation comes about, the paragraph has unity. Each of the sentences in the paragraph uses *student*, or its substitute *he*, as the subject; therefore the paragraph maintains coherence through a consistent point of view. There are no mechanical errors.

Now, look at the second developmental paragraph.

> [1]In addition to being deprived of accurate presentations of literature, each time the student resorts to the comic classic version of a novel he misses practice in critical reading and evaluation of literature. [2]The student has no concept of the underlying theme of a particular story or of persistent themes that recur in one author's works. [3]Since the comic classics present only what the characters say, the reader has no way of interpreting the author's purpose for writing a story. [4]Further, since symbolism and point of view cannot be adapted to comic book presentation, the reader misses these artistic devices. [5]Finally, the student fails to see the structure of the novel because the emphasis is always on plot and action. [6]Regard-

less of the importance of setting or characters in the original version, the student will see plot as the dominant factor.

Again, in this paragraph, the first sentence is the topic sentence. The pointer is *misses practice*; the remainder must show why this practice is missed. The paragraph is developed through reason, and three reasons are given to indicate the validity of the topic sentence. The first is in the second sentence—the student misses the underlying theme or themes that recur in one author's work. The second reason is in the fourth sentence—the student misses symbolism and point of view. The third reason is in the fifth sentence —the student misses the structure of the novel because emphasis in classic comics is on plot and action only.

The paragraph maintains unity. The three reasons given directly support the topic sentence. The other sentences also contribute to the unity of the paragraph. The third sentence, for instance, explains the first reason given in the second sentence, and the sixth sentence explains the third reason given in the fifth sentence. The paragraph holds together well. The subject of each sentence is *student* or a pronoun or noun standing for student. To increase coherence, transition words are used twice. *Further*, in the fourth sentence, introduces the second reason, and *finally*, in the fifth sentence, introduces the third reason. Note further that the first part of the first sentence is used as transition to link this paragraph with the preceding one to improve the coherence of the whole paper.

Now consider the final paragraph.

[1]Of equal importance to the student who substitutes the comic classic version for the original novel, he does not enjoy the power and majesty of the English language as it has been used by our greatest authors. [2]He finds no new and interesting words to challenge him. [3]Because these books are intended primarily for a young, nonliterary audience, he encounters only simple, everyday words that he already knows. [4]Comparing the comic version with the author's, he finds the vocabulary confined to words with little, if any, connotative meaning. [5]The student will also find that most descriptive passages have been eliminated or reworded. [6]The author has described the actions and scenes in vivid, carefully chosen words, but the comic book reader sees only the crude and oversimplified drawings. [7]He discovers that he need not use his imagination to create a character because he has access to the stereotyped picture drawn by the comic strip artist. [8]Thus, he does not need the

figurative language that enriches and encourages imagination. [9]Not only does the student miss the artistry of word choice and description, he cannot see the different combinations of words in sentences and sentences in paragraphs used by authors to create distinctive styles. [10]Since he is reading a condensed and altered version of the novel, he is not aware of the vividness of an author's use of dialect or his ability to make the most ordinary things seem out of the ordinary. [11]He misses the artistry of an author like Poe who chose words for sounds and then placed these words in sentences, almost rhythmic and poetic. [12]By reading this inaccurate presentation of the world's great literature, the student denies himself the opportunity of reading the literature of the past, the value of developing a critical attitude toward literature, and the pleasure of enjoying the power and beauty of his own language.

This paragraph, as do the other developmental paragraphs, starts with the topic sentence. The point it develops is that the student who reads comic classics as substitutes for the real thing misses the power and majesty of the English language as used by the greatest authors. The developmental method is the use of detail—the piling up of reasons for what the student misses. The last sentence is the concluding statement. It contains the three reasons for the validity of the thesis statement that make up the topic sentences of the paragraphs.

Again, this paragraph is coherent and unified. All the sentences directly support the topic sentence. All the sentences use *student*, or the pronoun *he*, as subject. Notice, too, the use of the transition words *also*, in the fifth sentence, and *thus*, in the eighth sentence. Further, the beginning of the ninth sentence, *Not only does the student miss the artistry of word choice and description*, provides transition to the next group of ideas. The first part of the topic sentence, *Of equal importance. . . ,* connects this paragraph with the preceding one.

A diagram will demonstrate the overall organization of the whole paper.

Thesis statement:	Students cheat themselves when they choose the "easy way" of reading classic comics instead of required books.
Reason 1: (Topic Sentence)	They deny themselves an accurate presentation of the original story.

Reason 2:   They miss the opportunity to practice critical
(Topic Sentence)   reading and evaluation of literature.

Reason 3:   They lose enjoyment of the power and majesty
(Topic Sentence)   of the English language.

This paper could be marked *good* on organization, *good* on content, and *good* on mechanics, and it should earn a *good* grade.

When you write a five-hundred-word paper, it will need a title; so far, nothing has been said about titles. These eight guidelines will serve you well:

1. Use no more than five words.
2. Use no final mark of punctuation.
3. Make no reference to your title in the first lines of your paper.
4. Capitalize the first and last words of your title. Do not capitalize articles (a, an, the) conjunctions (and, but, or, and so forth), or prepositions, unless they have over five letters.
5. Make your title honest. (Do not try to be "cute.")
6. Summarize your paper in the title.
7. Do not make your title a sentence.
8. Never put quotation marks around your own title.

Take, for example, the title of the paper just analyzed. "The Student and Classic Comics." It requires only five words, has no final mark of punctuation, and has all words capitalized except the conjunction *and*. It is an honest title; it summarizes the paper; and it is not a sentence. It fulfills the requirements for a good title.

Now look at another paper.

THE LIBRARY, THE TEACHER, AND THE STUDENT

Students in the high school I attended have certainly lost the inquiring mind, if they ever had it, and they no longer even want to think for themselves. It seems, in fact, that our whole society has lost the zest for inquiry because of the loss of ideals and qualities. I cannot account for society's loss, but among students in my school I can see at least two reasons: inadequate libraries and prejudiced teachers.

This introductory paragraph is not bad. All the parts are there, but they are not organized. The first sentence is apparently the thesis statement. But this sentence is composed of two independent clauses: *Students in the high school I attended have certainly lost the inquiring mind* and *they no longer even want to think for themselves.* You have learned that this construction is not acceptable for a thesis statement because the clauses carry equal weight and there is no way for the reader to determine which is the subject of the paper. If you look at this sentence closely, however, you will realize that its author is saying the same thing in both parts. What he intends to be his thesis statement is that students no longer want to think for themselves. This idea should be given the important position in the sentence; it should be placed at the end of the first paragraph with the two reasons given in the third sentence, because they are apparently going to be used as topic sentences in the paper. The second sentence in the introductory paragraph is a general statement about all people, not just students, and it needs to be recast and used as the first sentence of the paragraph. But take care in recasting to avoid such general words as *ideals* and *qualities,* because as they are used in the second sentence, they are not specific enough to be meaningful. Even so, this paragraph holds together. Note that *lost* in the first sentence is repeated in the second and that it appears as *loss* in the third. All three sentences are tied together by repetition of a key word. The whole paragraph, however, could use some reorganization.

The first developmental paragraph discusses the first reason students do not want to think for themselves.

> In my high school, the library was pathetically inadequate. If we wanted to know about the latest scientific developments, we had no reference books to examine except a fifteen year old encyclopedia more suitable for the primary grades than for the high school. We could read no recent scientific magazines, because there were none, not even any fifteen years old. The most weighty current magazine in the library was the *Reader's Digest,* hardly the one in which to research a topic in, say, biology. If we were interested in literature, about the best we could do for modern fiction was *Seventeen* by Booth Tarkington or perhaps *The Virginian.* No teacher of any subject ever assigned us library work or outside reading. On the few occasions one of us did venture into the library on his own initiative, old Miss Spence, who had been librarian for twenty years, made it clear that she could not care less. If we came into the library, it only meant trouble for her. Under these conditions it is not surprising that the students did little inquiry into the

important problems of man. They did not even know what these problems were; they had no way of knowing.

This paragraph appears to be a good one. It starts with a topic sentence that has a pointer, *pathetically inadequate*. Basically, it gives three reasons in support of the validity of this topic sentence: (1) resources for scientific research were nonexistent; (2) literary research, particularly modern, was equally difficult; and (3) the teachers and the librarian were uninterested in encouraging library work. Each reason is supported by illustration, and the paragraph ends with a summary sentence. The paragraph reads well as a unit. Note, for instance, the repetition of *fifteen* in the first part of the paragraph and of *library* and *librarian* in the last part to help in achieving coherence. Unity is maintained because all the evidence offered supports the topic sentence.

Here is the last paragraph.

[1]We have modified our society a great deal in the past few decades. [2]With the new advances in knowledge and in working and living conditions, we have come to expect more from other people than from ourselves. [3]Students revel in the new prosperity, buying things, having fun, and joining clubs. [4]The sole aim of their lives has become to have pleasure, so much so that they simply do not have time for school or studies or satisfying their natural curiosity. [5]In fact, they do not even notice these things, because they do not contribute to what they consider their pleasure. [6]Teachers foster this pursuit of pleasure in their students by trying to make their students all conform to what they think students ought to be and to think. [7]Students are expected to parrot on quizzes the ideas the teacher has given out in class. [8]They do not want us to think for ourselves but to go to established authorities for even simple ideas and explanations. [9]These teachers, and other forces in society, who rebel against nonconformity (something may or may not be right, but they won't try to find out if it is or not) make certain that a teacher with other ideas is not allowed to exist in their little world. [10]This is well illustrated by the case of Mrs. Jane Doe, a former teacher of mine. [11]In her English classes, she discussed everything, always taking the view opposite that of the majority of her students. [12]She would rant in class in her attacks on the established order of society or politics or tradition, and actually spoke in favor of Communism just to get her students to argue with her. [13]Her attacks forced her students to think to support their views. [14]Forcing her students to think was the best thing she did for her students. [15]But Mrs. Doe was accused of being a Communist and fired because the

other teachers, the school administrators, and the community did not appreciate her value. [16]With the lack of research facilities in the school library and with this sort of narrow-mindedness from our teachers, students at the high school I attended cannot think for themselves.

This paragraph is a jumble of ideas without unity, and what seemed to be a promising paper falls to pieces. The introductory paragraph announces that the paper will develop two reasons for the validity of the thesis statement: Students do not want to think for themselves because (1) the library is inadequate and (2) the teachers are prejudiced. This paragraph should be the one that develops the pointer *prejudiced*, but the word does not even appear in the paragraph.

What has happened to this student? He may have started writing the paper without thinking it through. Then when he reached this last paragraph, he was not sure what he would use to support his idea about the teachers being prejudiced. Rather than going back and reorganizing—not much change needed—he plunged ahead and ruined his paper. Or, he may have failed to see that his last paragraph discusses two subjects, not one. He changes direction in the middle of the paragraph. Through the fourth sentence, the paragraph has to do with the hectic life students lead and how it stops them from thinking. The remainder of the paragraph, however, is concerned with teachers' narrow-minded conformity and the way it restricts student thinking. Each of the two main ideas should have been developed in a separate paragraph. This paragraph is a good example of the use of hazy, undefined terms *(advances in knowledge and in working and living conditions, forces in society)* that allow the writer to wander off in all directions with no particular point being supported.

The third paragraph might be questioned at several points. The trouble is largely a matter of diction—the use of hazy, general words instead of specific ones that convey exact meaning. For instance, look at the beginning of the second sentence: *With the new advances in knowledge and in working and living conditions. . . .* What precisely does the general term *advances* mean to the writer? How does he intend for the reader to know what he means? We can guess at the meaning, but we cannot be certain. In addition, how have these *advances* led us *to expect more from other people than from ourselves?* Because the writer does not answer this question and he does not define *advances,* the sentence seems meaningless. The instructor might mark this sentence simply with a question mark in the margin. If you should see this mark on your paper, it indicates that the reader cannot determine what you mean and that in revision you need to clarify.

The seventh sentence will also have to be questioned. It begins *These teachers, and other forces in society, who rebel against nonconformity (something may or may not be right, but they won't try to find out if it is or not). . . ,* and stops the reader cold. He cannot possibly continue into the sentence after this point without rereading this beginning carefully to determine precisely what is being said. The parenthetical material is confusing; something is being defined, but what? Further, the sentence introduces a new subject, *other forces in society,* that appears irrelevant to the discussion. The dependent clause following this phrase, *who rebel against nonconformity,* is twisted in such a way that the reader must stop to figure it out. Ordinarily, we speak of rebelling against conformity rather than against nonconformity. We rebel against what is established. Nonconformity could hardly be said to be the established way of life in our society. So the reader is confused by this clause. *Who support conformity* is a much better way of saying it here.

The illustration of the teacher who refused to conform is not a satisfactory one. It makes the reader wonder whether the school board was not perhaps justified in firing the teacher. She was apparently hired to teach English, but the illustration suggests that she taught everything but English. If she *ranted* in her classroom, it would make the school board's case more secure. But maybe this is another instance of the writer's difficulty in choosing precise words.

Read the next paper all the way through before any comment.

EXERCISE IN OUR DAILY LIVES

Exercise should play a very large role in daily life. Everyone, no matter what age, needs exercise every day. However, with modern life being what it is, few older people get the daily exercise they need. Probably television as well as other modern inventions play a part in producing the physically unfit American.

There are many kinds of exercise that will help people keep physically fit, if they are done every day. First, there are setting-up exercises that anyone can perform for a few minutes every day. If more people would do setting-up exercises on a regular schedule, fewer people in America would be sick. Younger people need to play games to keep themselves physically fit. Football is one of the best games a young person can play for this purpose. But any game that requires running and bending and stretching will do the same thing. Of course, young people should take advantage of the athletic programs in their school and of the school gymnasium on every occasion. Body building centers are springing up all over the United States. In these centers, anyone from the youngest person to the oldest can set up an exercise program under the supervision of an expert in body building. Or, of course, a family can always buy exercise equipment such as stationary bicycles, barbells, and slant boards on which to exercise daily. If more people would exercise daily, they would find that they feel better all the time.

Television and other modern inventions could possibly be a factor that produces the physically unfit American. Television can be very educational. There are many educational programs for adults as well as for the young generation. "Face the Nation," for example, and news programs such as "CBS Reports" can help the people of the United States learn more about the advancing world. But mostly, television is just a waste of time, being concerned altogether with entertainment programs. Another modern invention that contributes to the physically unfit American is the automobile. People no longer walk any place. If they have to go only two blocks to the grocery store, they get in the car and ride there instead of walking. Even the young people don't walk, but expect their parents to give them a car at an early age. If people are going to sit for hours in front of their television sets and ride in their cars everywhere, they need to get exercise by doing setting-up exercises or working out on gym equipment.

In our progressing world, everyone seems to be looking for more and more entertainment and for easier ways of doing things. It is easier for a mother to have her children watch entertainment programs on television while she does her work around the house than it is to put her housework off while she takes her children outside for some healthy exercise or outdoor play. By doing this is the mother making things easier for herself or is she thinking about her children's welfare? A good mother will let her children play outdoors while she does her housework. Under the same conditions, adults will watch television rather than exercise as they should.

You recognize at once that the paper is poor, and you are able to point out its chief weaknesses. If an instructor attempts to mark everything unacceptable in this paper, the margins will not accommodate his marks and comments. Perhaps personal conferences with the instructor will guide this student writer.

One of the chief weaknesses of this paper is its content. The very title, "Exercise in Our Daily Lives," suggests emptiness and dullness. When the reader sees the thesis statement, *Exercise should play a very large role in daily life,* the first sentence, he knows the paper will not be vital. First, *very large* is not precise. How much exactly is a *very large role?* Second, who wants to read about so commonplace a subject, one that everyone knows about already?

Despite the confusion apparent in the introductory paragraph, the reader may discern three points the paper uses to support the thesis: (1) everyone needs exercise every day; (2) few older people get the daily exercise they need; and (3) television and other modern inventions produce the unfit American. None of these supports the thesis statement as given. We need go no further into the paper than the brief introductory paragraph to predict the results—an unacceptable paper. The rest of the paper bears out such a prediction. The paragraphs are not unified. Each of them jumps from subject to subject, changing direction every sentence or so. Some second paragraph material is discussed in the third, and some in the third is discussed again in the fourth. Therefore, the paragraphs cannot be coherent; no use of coherence devices will help these paragraphs, unless they are first rewritten for unity. Diction and sentence structure will have to be revised. Some sentences, possibly the result of too little thought or too hasty revision, come out unintentionally humorous. Look, for instance, at the last sentence. The writer has just explained that many mothers allow their children to waste time watching television because it speeds up housework. The last sentence says: *Under the same conditions, many adults will watch television in their spare time.* The reader is tempted to counter, "Under what conditions? While their mother is taking care of them?"

WRITING ASSIGNMENT

1. Select one of the following general topics (your instructor may add to this list).

Dating
Parents
Politics
School
Sports

2. Restrict your selected general topic by dividing it into its parts and by choosing one of these restricted parts as suitable for development in a five-hundred-word paper.

3. Write a good thesis statement.

4. Decide on at least three reasons for the validity of the thesis statement. (Your instructor may want to check what you have done before you go on.)

5. In one paragraph, use reason as the basic method of development; in another, use either comparison or contrast; and in another, use illustration, either a series of short illustrations or one extended illustration. (Your instructor may substitute other methods for these.)

6. Underline your thesis statement and all topic sentences.

7. Write in the margin, beside each developmental paragraph, the principal method of development used in that paragraph.

Revising Your Paper—Diction

6

The first complete copy of your five-hundred-word paper is the rough draft. At this point, you will have managed merely to get organized ideas and evidence down on paper. Next, you must go back over your paper slowly and thoroughly, checking on unity, coherence, and convincing support of thesis statement and topic sentences. Mark out and change words and lines liberally as you see the need. Supply transition where you have neglected it in the first draft. Then make a copy of the paper as revised. Give this second copy the same close scrutiny that you gave the first, and make additional changes where needed. It may be necessary to make yet another copy before you are satisfied that you have produced a paper as polished and exact in idea as you can make it. Never turn in a paper that has not gone through this process of revision.

Manuscript neatness is not a virtue in itself. Sometimes students attempt to hide emptiness of thought and idea by precisely and neatly following a specified form. Usually, this attempt is unsuccessful. On the other hand, some students neglect form and neatness by concentrating only on content. This, too, makes an unsuccessful paper. Consider two points: Your reader (the instructor) will have many papers to read through and mark, a laborious process at best. Imagine his reaction when he has to waste time deciphering what the student has written. He may not let this influence the grade he puts on the paper, but he may, sometimes unconsciously. Why take the chance? Another point: No employer will tolerate messy work. You might as well get in the habit of doing it right.

Hopefully, after your first paper or so, you will become so conscious of what makes a good paper that you will avoid some of the effort of revision by using good writing practices in your first draft. Indeed, you must do this if time is short, as it certainly is in a fifty-minute class period. Here are some pointers to keep in mind when you are writing the first draft and when you are revising.

Change the Passive Voice to Active Voice

English verbs have two voices—active and passive. For example, consider these sentences:

Andy hit the ball.

The ball was hit by Andy.

The first sentence is in the active voice. The subject, *Andy*, is doing the action expressed in the sentence. The second is in the passive voice. The subject of this sentence, *ball*, is receiving the action. Or, to put it another way, the first sentence (active) follows the normal word order for English sentences—subject, verb, complement (or actor, action, receiver of action). The second sentence (passive) turns this normal word order around. What was the complement of the first sentence becomes the subject in the second sentence. Its order is receiver of action, action, actor.

Look at this example.

[1]To call a telephone on your own party line proceed as follows: Lift the receiver and wait for dial tone. [2]The regular seven-digit number of the desired station is dialed, the busy signal will be heard, and the calling party then places the receiver on the hook. [3]The desired station is then signaled. [4]After a reasonable time, remove receiver and start talking.

The author of these directions has shifted from active to passive and back to active in four brief sentences. The resulting jumble is enough to cause any telephone subscriber to hesitate calling a neighbor on his own party line. The first sentence is in the active voice. The subject *you*, the actor, is understood. *You* are to lift the receiver and *you* are to wait for the dial tone. The second sentence, however, shifts to the passive. There is no one dialing, and no one is hearing the busy signal. The last part of the second sentence shifts again to active voice. The calling party acts. Again, in the third sentence, no one is signaling the desired station, and the sentence is passive. The final sentence returns to the active voice with an understood *you* as the actor. These directions do not communicate clearly to the reader; they confuse him. If the understood *you* had acted throughout (that is, if the author had remained in the active voice), there would be no confusion about following the directions.

The passive voice is not always inappropriate, of course, or there would be no need to have it in the language. But it must be used where it is appropriate and where it is unobtrusive. If, for instance, you do not know who performs the action, or if the actor is too unimportant to the thought of the sentence to be worth mentioning, it is often appropriate to use the passive verb. If you write, "Highway 6 was completed last May," no one is going to insist that you change this passive construction into an active one by naming the engineering firm that built the road. But you probably do not need to leave this sentence in the passive voice. You can easily make it a phrase and put it into a longer, active sentence, for example: "Highway 6, completed last May, has increased trade in Boonville by fifty per cent," or "Completion of Highway 6 last May boosted trade in Boonville."

This example has acceptable use of the passive voice.

> After the operation, Ernest was moved to his room and was given a sedative by the nurse who was to watch over him during his long convalescence.

In this sentence, we can take it for granted that a doctor performed the operation and that an orderly moved Ernest to his room. There is no point in mentioning them, for they are unimportant in this context. Notice that the remainder of the sentence continues in the passive, *was given by the nurse,* instead of *the nurse gave.* This use of passive is appropriate because to change it to active would change the point of view in mid-sentence. To make it active, this part of the sentence would have to become an independent clause preceded by a comma: . . . room, *and the nurse who was to watch over him during his long convalescence gave him a sedative.* A second objection to this active form of the verb is the distance between the subject of the clause, *nurse,* and its verb, *gave.* Ordinarily, they should be as close together as possible. Here they are too far separated.

The passive, then, can be used with care when the actor is unknown or unimportant or when the active voice would interfere with style or cause a clumsy construction. Usually, you should change any passive sentences to active ones. Sometimes students use passive constructions to avoid using the first person *I.* For example, sentences such as this one appear frequently: *C. Goehring's* Life in the Jungle *was selected for a book report because of the interest of its subject matter to this reader.* Note that no one has selected a book in this sentence. *This reader* may have, but who is he? Better by far to say in a forthright manner: *I selected C. Goehring's* Life in the Jungle *for a book report because its subject matter interested me.* Furthermore, do not refer to yourself in writing as "the author" or "this writer." Attempting to avoid the first person almost always leads to a poor use of the passive or to clumsy circumlocutions.

Here are more examples of poor use of the passive taken from student papers.

Coffee had to be drunk and cookies eaten before games were played. (No one in this sentence is doing anything. Change to something like: The visitors had coffee and cookies before playing checkers and monopoly.)

Games to be played were checkers and monopoly. (Again, no one is playing the games. Make it active this way: They will play checkers and monopoly.)

8:15 was shown by the clock on the wall. (Very simple to change. The clock should be doing the action expressed here, so make it the subject of the sentence: The clock on the wall showed 8:15.)

EXERCISE

Change any passive construction to active in these sentences.

1. Her skirts were always too short, Jane's parents insisted, and when she got a veto on her white leather suit, tears were shed, enough to fill Thompson's creek.
2. When the fourth child came, all plans to move to Bardtown in the spring were given up by the Guy family.
3. More than ten pounds of fish and sixteen sacks of ten-cent peanuts were consumed by the two dieting spinsters per week on their carbohydrate diet.
4. In 1910, his case was called incurable by every doctor in the north woods of Maine.
5. "All that I hope to be, I owe to my beloved oilwell," was the twist Miss Susie gave the Lincoln quote.
6. The centerpiece was arranged by the office secretary, while doughnuts and coffee were set out on card tables in the foyer by the clerk-typist.
7. Plans to attend the first session of summer school were made by the Douglass girls.
8. The hay was thrown over the fence by Farmer Swenson, whose cows were then called by their owner to "Come and get it!"
9. J. R.'s closet held more than fifty sports shirts, but every time, he chose the blue-gray plaid.

10. The house on Suffolk Street was pink and brown with a most vulgar green on the roof, and the color combination was loudly bemoaned by the neighborhood, as it was by the new owner.
11. Facts could not be ascertained, and so no decision was reached by the Committee to Remove Uncooperative Members from the club rolls.
12. Lee pranced home to stun his father with the news that he would be blasting off to California for the summer with the guys.
13. Complaints were heard by the young man when he announced to his parents that he had just quit his new job.
14. The mystery of the missing hymnals was finally solved by the rector at the Saturday meeting of the acolytes.
15. Because of the development of seven new cavities, the afternoon was unpleasantly spent in the dentist's office.
16. Excellent recommendations were given on the application sent by the artist from Arkansas.
17. The practice was continued until the target was hit by every marksman.
18. On November 15, agreement was reached among the Brechner Boulevard neighbors over rights to the water tank.
19. Amazing progress has been made by the Bell County Chamber of Commerce.
20. All the potato salad, as well as the Greek olives and the pickles, were eaten before mid-afternoon.

Avoid Listless Verbs

They deaden your writing. As you revise, change as many of these as possible to lively verbs.

ARE	GO
IS	SAY
IT IS	SEE
HAD	THERE ARE
HAS	THERE IS
HAVE	

Look at the italicized verbs in this paragraph.

The Volkswagen *is* unexcelled for dependability. It *is* well-behaved under driving conditions in which other cars *are* kept off the road. Unlike conventional cars with their engine over the front wheels, the VW engine *is* in the back, which gives superior traction to the rear wheels. As a result, the VW can *climb* steep, slippery hills with ease or it can *go* with sureness through ice, snow, mud, and sand.

Furthermore, other cars *are* easily outperformed by the VW even under the most extreme temperature conditions because *there are* no radiator problems in the VW. The VW engine *is* air-cooled; thus *there are* no leaks, rust, or antifreeze problems peculiar to conventional cars. Any time, summer or winter, day or night, the VW *is* ready to go anywhere.

Every verb in this paragraph, with the exception of *climb*, is on the list. Further, a poor use of the passive appears in mid-paragraph. Can you spot it? It marks a change in point of view.

This paragraph as it stands is not the worst one ever written, but making it better is simple. Just change the verbs (automatically taking care of the passive construction).

Unexcelled for dependability, the Volkswagen *behaves* well under driving conditions that *frighten* other cars off the road. Unlike conventional cars with their engines over the front wheels, the VW, with its engine's weight in the back of the car, *allows* the rear wheels superior traction. As a result, the VW *climbs* steep, slippery hills with ease or *cruises* securely through ice, snow, mud, and sand. Further, the VW outperforms other cars even under the most extreme temperature conditions, because it *needs* no radiator. The air-cooled engine thus *develops* no leaks, rust, or antifreeze problems peculiar to conventional cars. Any time, summer or winter, the VW *stands* ready for anything.

In this revision, none of the listless verbs appear. No change in point of view mars the paragraph's coherence. No weak use of the passive confuses the reader.

Occasionally, you will find it necessary to use some of the listless verbs. Fine! As long as you do not overuse them to the point that your writing becomes boring. A good rule to follow is: *Change any verb that does not draw a picture.*

EXERCISE

Change all colorless verbs in these sentences to stronger, active ones.
1. The tour conductor said that we could not lean over the wooden railing.
2. There is a fat little green pig with roses on his back placed on the dresser.
3. The painter came down the shaky ladder and put his pan and brush down on the floor in disgust.

4. The driver drove his truck down the road, passing cars on the icy road very carelessly.
5. The girl was crying when she said that the police were after her.
6. The governess could see the dusting powder all over the floor, and some of it was on the bedspread and some on the study table.
7. Sylvia gave a loud cry when she realized that the telephone call was long distance from her sister Laura in Philadelphia.
8. Every time one of the carbonated drinks was opened, out came a gush of purple pop with a hissing noise, and I had to put it down and run to keep from getting wet from the spray.
9. Jackson had a stomach-ache, so he said, and he told us that there were six other leading athletes who had stomach-aches, too.
10. We went first to Los Angeles and then went on to Kansas City, not getting to the convention until Thursday afternoon.

Examine All Uses of "Who" and "Which"

The overuse of *who* and *which* weighs writing down with deadwood (that is, unnecessary words). These words introduce dependent adjective clauses. Almost always the clauses can be reduced to phrases with a resulting economy in wording and increase in interest. Here is an example.

> Terry's *Guide to Mexico*, which was first written over fifty years ago, has gone through nine revisions, of which the latest was in 1965.

If you drop the first *which* and the first *was*, along with the *of which* and the same listless *was*, you will have a stronger and more economically worded sentence.

> Terry's *Guide to Mexico*, first written over fifty years ago, has gone through nine revisions, the latest in 1965.

In the next two sentences, the *who* and *which* are unnecessary.

> Jack Jones is a man who calls every trick. (Let us assume from his name that Jack Jones is a man. Then strike *is a man who,* and you have cleared away four words of deadwood. Yet the meaning is intact.)

> Jack Jones calls every trick.

> Peterson's poem, "The Way to Heaven," is a poem which needs no explanation. (As in the previous sentence delete *is a poem which* and you have eliminated a weak *is* and an unnecessary *which.*)

> Peterson's poem, "The Way to Heaven," needs no explanation.

Note the number of who's, which's, listless verbs, and other dead-wood in this paragraph.

1   The University catalog *can be used* to good advantage by the
2 freshman *who is* bewildered by university life. *It is* revised every
3 year *in order that* it *will be* up-to-date. First *of all, there is* in this
4 catalog a list of all the courses *which are* offered by the University.
5 These courses *are* arranged alphabetically by department *in order*
6 *that* the student may choose *which* courses he wants to take. *It is*
7 *also* from this list *of* courses *of* each department that a degree
8 plan for the student *can be* devised, *which will be* within the
9 limits *of* the regulations *of* the University.

Line 1: Listless verb, *can be used.*

Line 2: A *who* followed by the listless verb *is.* Write it *the freshman bewildered by university life* and avoid both. *It is* at the beginning of the next sentence needs revision. Why not leave this whole sentence out and substitute the one word *current* before *University* in the first line?

Line 3: Listless verb *will be.* Problem avoided if you delete this whole sentence as suggested. *First of all.* Do not use this expression. If you must use a *first,* be certain you also use a *second.* In any case, delete *of all.* Do not use *firstly* or *secondly* at any time.

Line 4: *Which* followed by listless verb *are* needs examination.

Line 5: Listless verb *are* needs revision. *In order that.* Do not use this phrase; . . . *to allow the student choice of courses* is better here.

Line 6: *Which* avoided by the revision suggested for line 5. *It is,* at the beginning of the next sentence, needs to be removed by revision.

Line 7: *Of courses of each department* has too many *of's.* Remove one *of* by writing *of departments' courses.*

Line 8: Listless verb *can be* needs changing. *Which* followed by listless verb *will be* also needs revising.

Line 9: *Of the regulations of the University.* Delete one *of* by writing *of University regulations.*

All lines: The passive construction in every sentence underlies most of the problems in the paragraph. The active voice will eliminate *which, who,* and listless verbs.

Here is a revision of the paragraph. Notice the difference in length when the deadwood is deleted.

The current University catalog offers help for bewildered freshmen. It lists all University courses alphabetically by department, allowing the student, if he follows University regulations, to choose his own courses and devise his own degree plan.

Look now at a paragraph by Robert Louis Stevenson. Here no *which* or *who* clutters the thought. No overuse of listless verbs deadens it. Some passive constructions appear. Can you spot them? Verbs are italicized.

These long beaches *are* enticing to the idle man. It *would be* hard to find a walk more solitary and at the same time more exciting to the mind. Crowds of ducks and sea gulls *hover* over the sea. Sandpipers *trot* in and out by troops after the retiring waves, trilling together in a chorus of infinitesimal song. Strange seatangles, new to the European eye, the bones of whales, or sometimes a whole whale's carcase, white with carrion gulls and poisoning the wind, *lie* scattered here and there along the sands. The waves *come* in closely, vast and green, *curve* their translucent necks, and *burst* with a surprising uproar that *runs* waxing and waning, up and down the long keyboard of the beach. The foam of these great ruins *mounts* in an instant to the ridge of the sand glacis, swiftly *fleets* back again, and *is* met and buried by the next breaker.[1]

Three listless verbs appear in this paragraph—*are* in the first sentence, *be* in the second sentence and *is* in the last sentence, and these are all passive. But these are the only listless verbs and the only passive constructions in the paragraph. Notice the preponderance of strong, active verbs—*hover, trot, lie, curve, runs, burst, mounts, fleets.* Note also the absence of *which* and *who.*

EXERCISE

Revise the following sentences to eliminate *who, which,* listless verbs, and other deadwood.

1. Bill decided to take the road to the east, which would get him to Troy fifteen minutes sooner.
2. Grace sold the book which had been given to her last Christmas in order to buy a ticket to Calico Rock.
3. Geoffrey Chaslin, who played the lead in *A Man for All Seasons,* which is a play about Sir Thomas More, visited London last year in order to become better equipped to play the role.

[1]Robert Louis Stevenson, in "The Old Pacific Capital," first published in *Frazier's Magazine,* November, 1880.

4. His grandfather, who is also his godfather, gave him an air rifle, which his parents stole and hid, he said.
5. The tall elm tree, which had replaced the scrubby oak, lost all its leaves and turned sick, which worried Frances, who had done all she could to keep the homestead pretty.
6. She decided to wear the black and white pique, which her mother made and which was far prettier than any of the others wore, which included Sharon, whose dad is Dean of Everything on campus.
7. He went through all of the cancelled checks of the Bank of Commerce in order to try to find the one which he had sent to the mortgage company to make his house payment for the month of January.
8. Joe McCown is the man who contributed all his ranch income to the orphan whom the police found in the house which was deserted. (Note: If you have to use them, how do you decide bewteen *who* or *whom*? It is simple. *Who* and *whom* will be found only in dependent clauses. Remove the clause from the sentence and substitute *he* or *him* in place of the *who* or *whom*. If *he* fits, then *who* is proper; if *him* fits, choose *whom*. For example, in this sentence *who* is found in the clause *who contributed his ranch income*. If you try both *he* and *him* in place of the *who*, you will find that the only *he* will properly fit: *He contributed his ranch income*. So *who* is correct here. *Whom* is found in the clause *whom the police found*. You will find that only *him* can be substituted for *whom*: *The police found him*. So *whom* is proper in this clause. If it is plural, substitute *they* for *who* or *them* for *whom*.)
9. The choice which was made was between Bill and him, neither of whom had any experience in typing, which was required of the person who was to be employed. (Is this *whom* proper?)
10. There is no reason for the chairman, who is Philip Jones, to take offense at the motion, which is aimed at electing a vice-chairman who is to help him with his duties.

Avoid Anything Trite

Some words and phrases are used so much that they become worn out. Yesterday's slang, for instance, is trite today. Not many of you would want to "cut a rug" or to "put a bee" in someone's "bonnet," nor would many now use a phrase like "crazy, mixed-up kid." These are out of date. The same happens to certain combinations of ordinary words, as in these sentences.

He not only started sweeping like mad, but also gave me a list of items to buy for the party, such as the following: party hats, confetti, horns, and so forth. These things proved to be so much fun that we had a ball.

The trite words and expressions are listed below.

Not only . . . but	And so forth
Like mad	Proved to be
Such as	We had a ball
The following	Items

Or Any Exhausted Phrase

Each of these sentences contains at least one exhausted phrase, a phrase that is used over and over. They are *italicized*. Avoid them and others like them.

Due to the fact that I had gained too much weight in the past month, I *turned down* his invitation to dinner. (Always substitute *because* for *due to the fact that*. It works every time.)

This apathy has spread over the *entire world*. (Why not just *world?*)

Our ever-growing population will be a problem in *just a few short years*.

To this rule I was no exception.

We crossed the street *in order to* avoid meeting him. (We crossed the street to avoid meeting him. Always delete *in order.*)

In this fast moving world, the scientist must *keep abreast of* technological advances.

In this land of ours today, no one can really be a *rugged individualist.*

So for many years to come we will feel the effect of Sputnik.

Yes, truly it can be said that young people today are rebellious.

Ours is becoming a *push-button society.*

Texas Avenue will soon reach the limit of its capacity, *as far as* traffic *is concerned.* (A particularly poor one.)

These expressions only fill space. They add nothing to the thought of the sentence. Avoid them *like the plague* (another one!).

EXERCISES

A. Pick out all trite and exhausted words and phrases in this paragraph.

Yes, truly the American way is the one which is best suited to serve the needs and desires of the people of this far-flung world of ours today. Even if one of the various and sundry philosophies which oppose our way of life were to win out and conquer our country as well as all others, there are various means through which we could make a comeback. We could pull the rug out from under our enemies by stirring up a hornet's nest of far-flung, ever-increasing destruction of enemy materiel, that is, as far as their supply lines are concerned—trains, airplanes, and so forth—so that they would not have a leg to stand on, as far as fighting us is concerned. It would, therefore, prove to be the case that in order to keep us under their thumb, our enemies would have discovered that they have bitten off more than they can chew and would be facing an impossible task.

B. Rewrite these sentences with a fresh approach so that exhausted words and phrases are removed.
1. She had clearly suffered the ravages of time.
2. We sat under the sheltering arms of the gnarled old oak.
3. Would you believe half a million trading stamps?
4. He is twenty-three and not getting any younger.
5. Heaven only knows and time will tell which way the cookie crumbles.
6. She is the motherly type and talks to me like a Dutch uncle.
7. She left no stone unturned to find happiness at any price.
8. He felt a fierce loyalty for his native Arkansas.
9. The little children played at games and such until dinner.
10. Restitution will be made by June 20.
11. When we asked him about the missing cookies he looked as guilty as the cat that ate the canary.
12. When the going got rough, Becky decided to turn the job over to Susan.
13. He soon discovered that a rolling stone gathers no moss and settled down to a steady job.
14. In my opinion, I think he was just whistling in the dark all the time he was smiling like a Cheshire cat.
15. On the other side of the ledger is the fact that he was driving like a bat when the accident occurred.

Avoid Forcing Your Reader to Love It

If you grow too enthusiastic about your subject, you may stretch your reader's credibility by making statements intended to convince him of the worth of your subject. You are, in effect, attempting to force him to fall in on your side. These sentences do just that:

Horseshoes is a delightful game that can always be enjoyed by everyone, young and old. (Maybe horseshoes is delightful, but there is *no* game that *everyone* will *always* enjoy.)

There's nothing as exciting as a good football game. (To some people there may be activities that are considerably more exciting— reading a book, for instance.)

Irma's Last Love is the most fascinating book ever written. (To the writer, but perhaps not to his reader.)

No one will regret making this trip into the depths of Devil's Canyon. (Not even the fellow who slips and breaks a leg on the descent?)

The point: Do not tell your reader how wonderful something is; make him feel it through the quality of your writing. Then you will not need to tell him.

Do Not Preach

"Preaching" usually takes the form of moralizing in writing. Rarely does a reader want a lecture on what his moral positions should be or on what he should believe. If you present convincing evidence, you will not have to draw the moral conclusions so odious to the reader. Look at these examples of student moralizing.

Young people should try to understand their parents.

If we all love our country, no foreign ideology can ever take us over!

Everyone should strive to live a more moral life.

Students, awaken! We must not let our sacred traditions be taken away from us.

Examination of these "preachy" sentences discloses the use of certain words that make the sentences preachy. These words divide naturally into two classifications.

1. *False words.*

Always	Everything
Ever	Never
Every	Nobody
Everybody	No one

When you use these words without qualification you say something about everyone or everything in a class. Almost no conclusion about everyone or everything can be valid. You can write that everyone must die someday or that everyone has been born; but otherwise, someone, somewhere, proves the exception to most statements about all people. (Note that in this last sentence I carefully avoided writing that someone proves the exception to *all* statements about all people.) The ridiculousness of using these words becomes apparent when you see a sentence such as this one:

> Everybody always likes everything about every film that Hitchcock makes, and no one ever criticizes his techniques.

2. *Commanding words.* Such words as *must, ought to, should,* and *had better* demand obedience to the writer. Such admonishment is more likely to make the reader resentful of your ideas than receptive to them.

Avoid Stilted Wording

When a writer attempts to impress his reader by using big words and flowery phrases inappropriately, he is stilted in his writing. He goes out of his way to make a simple statement complicated by using longer words and more words than the thought warrants. The result is lack of communication because ideas are obscured rather than clarified by the clutter of words. Look at these examples and their simplifications:

> The consumption of alcoholic beverages among the younger generation is escalating. (Young people are drinking more.)
>
> Felicitations on the auspicious occasion of your natal day. (Happy birthday.)
>
> I desire to pen my memoirs. (I want to write an autobiography.)
>
> He matriculated with the earnest desire to graduate in three years, but due to certain problems that presented themselves, he was forced to accept a grade of failing in two courses of study and finally found it necessary to withdraw from two others, which left as a remainder only one course, on which his instructor awarded him a grade of *C—*. (Although he wanted to graduate in three years, he failed six hours, dropped three, and barely salvaged three in his first semester.)

EXERCISE

Revise all moralizing and stilted wording in these sentences.
1. The surgeon hesitated, his features drawn and sorrowful, as he approached to verify our deep and foreboding premonition that the

immediate ancestor of our parent was expected to expire before the sun rose to shine upon the world again.

2. Everyone should consume some of the leafy green products of the garden every day because of their nutritional value.

3. The happy cries of the darling children reached the ears of their delighted parents.

4. Despite warnings of friends and family, of the government, and even of the tobacco manufacturers themselves, Hubert continued to partake of tremendous amounts of nicotine.

5. His employment was terminated due to the fact that his employer felt that an excessive number of hours per day were being spent in other than gainful pursuits.

6. She has the ability to discuss at length any topic of conversation that is introduced, despite the fact that she sometimes is less than expert in the field under discussion.

7. And so in conclusion, let me say that we should all strive in unison to extirpate from our society the evils of gambling.

8. The babe still lay quietly, lost in slumberland, as the wee hours of the morning ticked on and sounds of dawn reached the ears of the drowsy parents.

Avoid "Fine Writing"

Some beginning writers believe that a fancy and elaborate style is elegant. Be warned that it is not. For instance, a freshman English student had difficulty understanding why her instructor marked her down when she wrote the following:

> Lush, well-maintained grounds combine with the harmonic grace of the buildings to give a deep majestic glow to the grounds. Flying everywhere, beautiful birds lend their melodious tones, while squirrels flit from tree to tree, chattering ecstatically.

In trying to be artistic, the student said nothing. English instructors usually call this "fine writing," and they are not giving it a compliment. A good rule to follow is this: Write briefly, plainly, and sensibly. Do not put on airs or use flowery words. Say what you mean.

Avoid "ly" Words

Most "ly" words are adverbs and modify verbs or adjectives. When used to modify a verb, the "ly" word allows the author to deaden his writing by selecting a listless verb instead of searching for the strong active verb to make his writing more lively. For instance, you could write "He ate voraciously," but "He gobbled his food" draws a better picture. Sometimes the "ly" words are unnecessary, as they are in these sentences:

I have completely exhausted my supply. (Delete *completely*. If you have exhausted it, it is exhausted. There is nothing more to say.)

There was really no reason for his success. (Delete *really*. It is a filler word, as are most of the "ly" adverbs.)

His remarks were truly nonsense. (Delete *truly*. If they were nonsense, that is all there is to it. Another word used as a filler.)

There are some "ly" words you might want to avoid. Check your papers to be certain that you do not overuse these words.

absolutely	purely	unfortunately
completely	really	unquestionably
extremely	surely	
fortunately	truly	
positively	undoubtedly	

Avoid Vague Words

Vague words are those the writer can use from habit or without thought, as substitutes for specific words that convey exact meaning. Vague words convey little meaning because they are general. For instance, this sentence says nothing: "The many, different factors involved created various problems for many people." Nothing specific can be communicated to the reader through this sentence, and there is no point in writing it.

Here is a list of vague words to avoid. When you are tempted to use one of them, mark it out and select a more specific term.

a lot	factor	many	pretty
aspect	field (of)	much	provide
characteristic	innumerable	nice	several
consideration	interesting	people	thing (s)
contains	item	pertains	variety
deal	large	phase	various
different	lots of		very

It takes special effort for most beginning writers to avoid the words on this list, but the successful are rewarded. Remove these words from your vocabulary. Otherwise, you may end up saying nothing, as did the students who wrote these sentences:

> There are lots of ways to consider making a living.
>
> There are many and various sweaters to be made in all sizes and colors.
>
> The many different aspects of socialized medicine are interesting.

REVIEW EXERCISES

On the basis of the material in this chapter, revise these sentences in any way necessary.

1. World War II was over, and he was coming in on a wing and a prayer.
2. Marjorie Ann is gorgeous, but to hear her tell it, she is plain, unless she is too modest, as not many of her age group are.
3. He was on Cloud 9 when he inherited enough money to live in the manner to which he had become accustomed.
4. They know, moreover, that the malady was to be a lingering one and that insidiously it would increase in seriousness until the dear one's life itself would be snuffed out, as a candle is suddenly relieved of its light-giving pleasure when its usefulness is ended.
5. They were too tired to move, but they walked home, slowly as though they resented every step of it, but they did not have bus fare, and they did not know what else to do but to walk.
6. His own father, who was to Paul a financial wizard, and whom Paul hoped to imitate, knew now that the cards were down and that it would be tough sledding and uphill all the way from now on along the road to Wall Street.
7. To whom should she appeal for funds for the Scouting outing, she asked herself. Who cares enough to give, and from whom can I seek aid?
8. They hurried to church fast, because they knew that the choir director would not be happy if they came into rehearsal late again, and they did not like to walk the full length of the building up to the choir loft while she looked at them with anger in her eyes.
9. At least we can say with certainty that nobody can deny Charles the praise he deserves for making the organization run more smoothly than Tommy was able to, or Buster, either.
10. You haven't lived until you've sat at the lake's edge while the sun goes down, with a hired hand to mix up the refreshments and swat away the mosquitoes.

11. Freddie refused the invitation due to the fact that his aunt was expected, whom he had not seen since her third marriage, which was three years ago.
12. Nothing is more charming than Delilah with an armful of tulips and a smile on her face.
13. The doorbell had been loudly rung, and it was too late for anything but hope.
14. The figs preserved by Mrs. Wenglar, the ceramics painted and baked by Mrs. Hill, the doillies embroidered by Mrs. Pearl—all were truly lovely and all well deserved the blue ribbon.
15. The large family, including innumerable in-laws, showed interesting characteristics and aspects in lots of ways, especially as pertained to the various occupations and different hobbies they were involved in.

Revising Your Paper—
Sentences

7

THE SIMPLE SENTENCE

A sentence is not necessarily *a group of words containing a subject and a verb and expressing a complete thought.* Modern grammarians are cautious in defining a sentence, for the pat, conventional definition does not always fit. Perhaps it is best to think of a sentence as just a complete thought. Thus, single words like *help* and *incredible* can be sentences, when properly capitalized and punctuated, without our having to be concerned about what is understood; they are both units of expression.

Sentences come in all lengths: minute, medium, and mammoth. Some of the most effective in English are quite brief. For instance, the famous, shortest verse in the Bible, *Jesus wept*, expresses in its context more feeling and emotion than a longer sentence might. Similarly, at the end of *Hamlet*, Shakespeare uses four words, *The rest is silence.* On the other hand, sentences can be quite long. But extremely long sentences are used infrequently and only for a special effect that might not easily be conveyed by a series of shorter sentences. For instance, Ernest Hemingway tried to give the feeling of a bullfight in 151 words.

> Cagancho is a gypsy, subject to fits of cowardice, altogether without integrity, who violates all the rules, written and unwritten, for the conduct of a matador but who, when he receives a bull that he has confidence in, and he has confidence in them very rarely, can do things which all bullfighters do in a way they have never been done before and sometimes standing absolutely straight with his feet still, planted as though he were a tree, with the arrogance and grace that gypsies have and of which all other arrogance and grace seems an imitation, moves the cape spread full as the pulling jib of a yacht before the bull's muzzle so slowly that the art of bullfighting, which is only kept from being one of the major arts because it is impermanent, in the arrogant slowness of his veronicas becomes, for the seeming minutes that they endure, permanent.[1]

[1]Ernest Hemingway, *Death in the Afternoon.* Reprinted with the permission of Charles Scribner's Sons from *Death in the Afternoon* by Ernest Hemingway. Copyright 1932 Charles Scribner's Sons; renewal copyright © 1960 Ernest Hemingway.

Ordinary sentences are much shorter than this one, for the reader has trouble following long involvements. Shorter units of thought, cast for the most part in normal English word order, are more desirable; the reader can recognize such sentences almost automatically. Lewis Carroll, the author of *Alice in Wonderland,* recognized this fact long ago when he wrote the nonsense poem "Jabberwocky."

'Twas brillig and the slithy toves
Did gyre and gimble in the wabe;
All mimsy were the borogoves,
And the mome raths outgrabe.

Even though you do not know what *toves* or *borogoves* look like, or what *brillig* and *slithy* mean, you can still easily recognize that this verse is made up of English sentences. You can spot these unknowns as parts of speech: *Brillig, slithy,* and *mome* are obviously adjectives; *toves, wabe, borogoves,* and *raths* are nouns; *gyre, gimble,* and *outgrabe* are verbs.

Any group of nonsense words arranged in the patterns of English sentences can be recognized as sentences, as long as articles and prepositions are real. Look at these different sentence patterns using nonsense nouns, verbs, and verbals:

The junbig cranned a biglou.
A biglou was cranned by a junbig.
Cranned by a junbig was a biglou.
After cranning a biglou, the junbig
zlon up the donnen.

Each of these represents a recognizable English sentence pattern. The first uses normal word order for English sentences.

NORMAL ENGLISH WORD ORDER
Subject .... Verb .... Object
or
Actor .... Action .... Goal
(The boy .... hit .... the ball.)

Most English sentences are written in this order with these parts, and there are often modifiers (words, phrases, or clauses) of any one or all the parts. For emphasis and sentence variety, the normal word order can be varied: *Up the stairs ran the girl* reverses normal word order. The subject comes in last position. Such a sentence used rarely is acceptable, but overused, it draws attention to itself, as any unusual word order does.

To be called complete, in the conventional sense, a sentence must have at least two of the parts indicated above—a subject and a verb. The subject may be understood (*you*); the verb may not. A complete sentence expresses ONE complete thought. If it has more than one, it is not unified, that is, it does not move in one direction but in as many directions as there are topics in the sentence. Look at this sentence:

> My car broke down twice on the way to the campus, and I spent all day Monday at registration.

Here there are two complete thoughts in two independent clauses. One complete thought has no necessary relationship to the other. In effect, they move in different directions. This sentence, then, has MORE THAN ONE complete thought; consequently, it is not a good sentence. For the same reason, neither is this sentence a good one:

> Iris Stone was a healthy girl who was born and bred in Tampa.

Here the dependent clause, *who was born and bred in Tampa*, has no necessary connection with Iris Stone's being a healthy girl. There are two topics here also, and each should be put in a sentence of its own.

On the other hand, a group of words without a complete thought is a sentence fragment. Look at these groups:

> We arrived at 8:00 o'clock. Before the game started.

The first of these is one complete thought. The second is not. The presence of *before* turns this group of words into a dependent clause and demands the addition of an independent, complete unit. We can add this dependent element to the end of the other group of words by replacing the period with a comma. Then the dependent clause (with its incomplete thought) it attached to a complete thought:

> We arrived at 8:00 o'clock, before the game started.

Look at these two groups:

He preached against three sins. Cards, whisky, and tobacco.

The second group is made up of three nouns and one conjunction, but it is missing a verb to express action. It has LESS THAN ONE complete thought. Because the first group of words is a complete sentence, the second group can be attached to it, as it obviously should be:

He preached against three sins: cards, whisky, and tobacco.

EXERCISE

Try your hand at spotting which of these nonsense word groups are complete sentences. Write *F* for fragments, *C* for complete sentences.

1. The junbig cranned a biglou.
2. The junbig cranning a biglou.
3. After the junbig had cranned a biglou.
4. There is the biglou the junbig cranned.
5. Since cranning a biglou, which was done by the junbig.
6. A biglou was cranned by the junbig.
7. The biglou being cranned by the junbig.
8. The biglou cranning junbig.

Emphasizing Words and Ideas in a Sentence

Ideas and words gain emphasis if they are placed in strong positions within the sentence. In normal word order of English sentences, the opening and the closing positions are most emphatic. For instance, look again at this simple sentence:

ACTOR	ACTION	GOAL
The boy	hit	the ball.

The most important words in this sentence are in the most important positions. Boy (the actor) and the ball (the goal) are the important key words. In this normal English sentence, *boy* opens the sentence, and *ball* closes it. The key words are then in the emphatic positions—the beginning and the end. The end position is stronger, however, because words and ideas in that position are the last ones the reader sees.

This diagram will illustrate the importance of sentence positions.

Here the three sentence positions are assigned weights to indicate their relative importance. The beginning position has been given a weight value of one pound; the middle position, five ounces; and the strong end position, five pounds. Now, by applying these weight values to the key words in a sentence, we can assign a weight to the whole sentence to indicate the strength of its emphasis. Look at this group of sentences.

1.	However, *she* was an excellent *cook*.	5 lbs., 5 oz.
2.	*She* was an excellent *cook*, however.	1 lbs., 5 oz.
3.	An excellent *cook she* was, however,	1 lbs., 5 oz.
4.	*She* was, however, an excellent *cook*.	6 lbs.
5.	An excellent *cook*, however, was *she*.	6 lbs.

These weights are assigned by taking the key words (*she* and *cook*) and giving them the value of the position in which they appear in the sentence. Thus, in the first sentence, *she* is in the middle position and gets a weight of only five ounces. *Cook*, in the end position, gets a weight of only five pounds. Together, the whole sentence has a value, then, of five pounds, five ounces. In this sentence, one of the important positions, the beginning of the sentence, is taken by the unimportant word *however*, suggesting that this transition word might be better buried in the middle of the sentence. The second has even less emphasis. *She* is in the beginning position for one pound, but *cook*, the other key word, is lost in the middle position and can be assigned an importance of only five ounces. The whole sentence, then, has a weight of only one pound, five ounces. In the third sentence, the position of the key words is reversed, and the value of the sentence remains the same as for the second sentence. The fourth sentence, however, has a different arrangement. *She* is in the beginning position and weighs one pound, whereas *cook* is in the end position and weighs five pounds. The whole sentence weighs six pounds, more than any other so far considered. The reason for this is that the two key words come in the two important sentence positions. Note that the transition word, *however*, is in the middle position where it does not detract from the impact of the sentence on the reader. The fifth sentence also puts the key words in the important positions, but the difference is that the positions have been switched. The sentence emphasis remains the same on the surface because it is assigned the same weight as the fourth sentence. But the two sentences differ considerably.

The fourth sentence is in normal English word order, which indicates that we ordinarily use this arrangement of sentence parts in writing. The fifth sentence reverses the arrangement, and the very oddness of this switch will make it more emphatic if it is mingled in a context of sentences arranged in the expected normal order. Only occasionally would you rely on a sentence like the fifth one—only when you want an unusual emphasis on the sentence. Although sentence variety is important, most of your sentences will have the same arrangement of sentence parts as that in the fourth sentence.

The Periodic Sentence

In any writing, the most powerful position for an idea—the one that gives the idea most emphasis—is at the end. In this respect, a sentence is no different from any other piece of writing. *The power spot in the sentence is at the end.* The main idea in a sentence, then, should come logically in this power spot. A sentence withholding its main idea until the end of the sentence is called *PERIODIC.* Look at this sentence:

Just as he bent over to tie his shoelace, *a car hit him.*

Here, the main idea, *a car hit him*, is at the end of the sentence. Certainly the other idea in the sentence is of less significance.

The Loose Sentence

More common in English, the *LOOSE* sentence ends with a dependent sentence element—a subordinate element. Rearranging the sentence just used as an example produces a loose sentence:

> A car hit him, *just as he bent over to tie his shoelace.*

The main clause (the independent clause) containing the main idea comes first in the sentence, whereas the subordinate element (the dependent clause) is at the end. Take care to keep the main idea in the main clause. If you do not, sentence emphasis goes askew. In this sentence, for instance, the insignificant idea is in the main clause, and the main idea is in a dependent clause:

> He bent over to tie his shoelace, just as a car hit him.

The first of the sentence is the main clause; the second part, the dependent clause. Such a sentence can have no logical emphasis.

Here are two more examples of a loose and a periodic sentence; the main idea is italicized in each.

> (Periodic) Having passed his house every day and knowing that it had been unoccupied for years, *I was surprised to see smoke coming from the chimney.*

> (Loose) *I was surprised to see smoke coming from the chimney,* because I had passed his house every day and knew that it had been empty for years.

Periodic sentences build suspense to gain emphasis for the main idea. If the main idea is held to the last in the sentence, and modifying elements are built up in the first part of the sentence, a marvelous suspense can be achieved that makes the main idea hit the reader with force. For instance, a simple sentence of this type makes little impact on the reader:

> The old woman fainted.

But we can add a dependent element before this sentence, make it periodic in tone, and increase its impact:

As confetti showered her head, the old woman fainted.

We can increase its impact even more by adding another dependent clause:

As the laughing crowd swirled around her and as confetti showered her head, the old woman fainted.

To heighten the impact yet further, add another dependent element:

As the band blared louder, as the laughing crowd swirled around her, and as confetti showered her head, the old woman fainted.

This type of periodic sentence is not as natural to the English language as it is to the modern Germanic languages. Most English sentences are loose in structure. That is, they are likely to be "strung" along with dependent elements at their end. They do not build to their point as the illustrative sentence above does. In English, the best sentences, then, are *periodic in tone but loose in structure.* You can achieve a periodic tone in three ways:

1. Suspending the subject.
2. Suspending the verb.
3. Suspending the complement.

To suspend an element, delay its appearance in the sentence.

1. *Suspending the subject.* Here is a sentence, simple in structure and English in word order:

The man hurried down the street.

Here the subject is *man.* To suspend this subject and give the sentence a periodic tone, delay the point where it appears in the sentence. Just add simple adjective modifiers before the subject:

The *gray-haired old* man hurried down the street.

Or you can add adjective phrases modifying *man:*

Limping on his wounded foot, the gray-haired old man hurried down the street.

You can suspend this subject even further by adding another phrase:

> Limping on his wounded foot and *staggering from side to side,* the gray-haired old man hurried down the street.

The sentence now has become periodic in structure as well as in tone. You can change the structure by adding modifying elements at the end:

> Limping on his wounded foot and staggering from side to side, the gray-haired old man hurried down the street that was littered with tin cans and shattered glass.

2. *Suspending the verb.* Using the same sentence and the same modifiers, you can delay the appearance of the verb in the sentence and create a periodic tone:

> The man *hurried* down the street. (Verb italicized)
> The man, *old* and *gray-haired,* hurried down the street. (Modifiers italicized)
> The man, *limping on his wounded foot,* hurried down the street. (Modifiers italicized)
> The man, *limping and staggering,* hurried down the street. (Modifiers italicized)

3. *Suspending the complement.* In this same sentence, you can also suspend the complement. The phrase *down the street* is not actually a complement in the strictest sense. It is not a noun construction but an adverbial prepositional phrase. The *complement* is used to mean a completer of the verb. *Down the street* fits this definition. Here it is suspended:

> The old man hurried *down the street.* (Complement italicized)
> The old man hurried *limping and staggering* down the street. (Modifiers suspending the complement italicized)

Caution: The process of suspending sentence elements can be overdone. If every element in the sentence is suspended, the subject, verb, and complement become too separated for the reader's quick comprehension of the thought. In the same way, take care not to separate any two elements enough to interfere with the flow of thought. The student who wrote this sentence, for instance, put too much space between the verb and the complement:

Chris attempted, even though his foot hurt him so much that he staggered as he ran, to reach the rifle.

In this sentence, the verb *attempted* and the complement (a verbal phrase), *to reach the rifle*, are separated by a long dependent clause. The result is a clumsy sentence so involved that the reader loses sight of the verb before he reaches the completer.

The Periodic-Loose Sentence

Consider these two sentences:

The ball soared toward the goalposts, which were fifty yards away from the kicker's toe. It wobbled end-over-end, but arced high and true.

Both sentences are concerned with one action, so they can easily be combined into one sentence. The second sentence can be reduced to two modifying phrases and worked into the first sentence. The first sentence would be improved by deleting the *which*. As the basic independent clause in the sentence, take this one:

The ball soared toward the goalposts.

Now, suspend the subject *ball* and the verb *soared* by adding modifying elements:

Arcing high and true, the ball, *wobbling end-over-end*, soared toward the goalposts fifty yards away.

Or, you can suspend the verb and the complement with these same modifiers:

The ball, *wobbling end-over-end*, soared *in a high and true arc* toward the goalposts fifty yards away.

These last two sentences are periodic-loose sentences because they have a periodic tone through the suspension of two sentence elements in the basic independent clause. The structure is loose because of the modifier *fifty yards away* at the end of the sentence.

EXERCISE

From each group of sentences, make one sentence by suspending two elements in the basic independent clause (italicized in each group).

1. *Bertha labored to secure bait to hook.* She winced as the worm tried to escape her uncertain grasp, and she hoped none of the other fisherman noticed her squeamishness.
2. *Ralph transported his aching jaws straight to the dentist's chair.* He held himself aloof with his shoulders erect as he marched through the reception room.
3. *The car coasted to a stop.* Its motor was dead. It bumped on one flat tire. It was long, shiny, and black.
4. *The legislature finally revoked the law.* The law had been impossible to enforce because the people held it in contempt. The legislature met in special session.
5. *The puppy barked at the cat.* He pranced and dodged back and forth. He was an excited puppy. The cat spat and hissed at him.
6. I hesitated for two weeks before making my choice, but I finally decided to attend Glory University. *I think I made the best choice.* I had to choose between Glory and Primitive University.
7. *Fleance broke up the rehearsal.* He entered from stage right. His wig was askew and his mascara was running. Lady Macbeth had just urged the assembly to "Take seats."
8. *The children giggled and cavorted.* They chanted "The Chinese flea keeps bugging me." They marched out of step and ill-aligned.
9. The English teacher looked the Salutatorian straight in the eye. She was angry. *She said, "When you chose that topic for your research paper, I told you it wasn't worthy of you."* The Salutatorian was embarrassed and crestfallen.
10. *Grandfather inched up the stairs.* He grasped the handrail with one hand. He leaned on his cane with the other. He firmly planted both feet on each step.

SECONDARY SENTENCE PATTERNS: COORDINATION AND SUBORDINATION

So far in this chapter you have dealt mostly with one type of sentence—the simple sentence with normal order (subject—verb—complement) and phrase and single word modifiers for one or more of the elements. In effect, you have been dealing with this pattern:

I see the puppy.

The idea expressed is approximately on the first grade level and is appropriate for a primer. But educated writers need to communicate more complicated ideas than this sentence pattern can express.

For this purpose, English provides secondary sentence patterns. The two most useful secondary sentence patterns are: (1) coordination (the simplest) and (2) subordination.

Coordination

Coordination is joining together like grammatical constructions with a connecting word called a conjunction. In its simplest form, two nouns or two verbs or two adjectives, for instance, can be joined by the conjunction *and*.

> Chris and Jane
> bacon and eggs
> read and write
> happy and carefree

Signal words for coordination (conjunctions)

Group 1.

> and
> but
> for
> nor
> or
> so
> yet

Conjunctions in this group can be used to join *equal* grammatical structures only. That is, they can join together two independent clauses, two noun clauses, two prepositional phrases, two participles, or two of anything, as long as they are the same grammatically. They cannot join together, however, an independent clause and a dependent clause.

Caution: Group 1 signal words, especially *and*, are sometimes inappropriately used to string sentences together. This relatively short sample uses *and* four times:

> I asked Dad for the car *and* then I picked up the corsage *and* got my date, *and* we went to the dance *and* had a wonderful time.

Although this sentence does have coordination, it defeats the purpose of coordination. Certainly there are no complicated ideas here that could not be expressed in the simplest sentence pattern.

Group 2.

consequently	nevertheless
hence	nonetheless
however	then
in fact	therefore
moreover	thus

These signal words are used as conjunctions *only* to join two independent clauses. They have no other use as conjunctions.

To illustrate the use of this group of conjunctions, here are two sentences:

> Marriage and hanging go by destiny. Matches are made in heaven.

Because these two are connected in idea, they may be joined grammatically into one sentence by making them independent clauses and by using a conjunction:

> Marriage and hanging go by destiny, *but* matches are made in heaven.

The Group 1 conjunction *but* is used here because a contrast is being drawn and this conjunction is the appropriate one. (Remember the section on transition words.) Or a Group 2 conjunction can be just as appropriately used:

> Marriage and hanging go by destiny; *however,* matches are made in heaven.

Or, the two sentences can be joined without a conjunction, if their ideas are closely enough related and if emphasis is needed:

> Marriage and hanging go by destiny; matches are made in heaven.

Punctuation of Coordinate Elements

Perhaps as many as sixty per cent of your punctuation problems can be solved by knowing the Group 1 and Group 2 conjunctions and by understanding how they work.

1. Group 1 conjunctions (*and, but, for, or, nor, so, yet*), when they join two independent clauses, take a comma before them. See the diagram below.

(Independent clause)   but   (Independent clause)
.... , ...

2. Group 2 conjunctions (*however, then, thus,* for instance) join two independent clauses together with a semicolon, in this way:

(Independent clause)   thus,   (Independent clause)
.... , ...

3. Two independent clauses may be joined without a conjunction if a semicolon separates them:

(Independent clause)   (Independent clause)
.... ;   ....

EXERCISES

Supply the proper mark of punctuation in the blanks of these sentences.

1. Great-grandfather would not refrain from chewing his noontime wad of tobacco .... nor would Great-grandmother give up dipping snuff, no matter how often we complained.
2. Santa brought Robin three dolls, a swing set, a Cinderella watch, and a plug-in refrigerator .... but Bobby seemed satisfied with his new socks and corduroy jeans.
3. The veteran scholar took his first degree in the history and literature of Persia .... the next step was to master the Arabic language.
4. From 6:00 to 10:00 in the evening he supplemented his income by teaching local teens to bowl .... so for eighteen hours a day he was on somebody's payroll.
5. Just before school opened, Old Hat found her way to Rita's doorstep .... and before Thanksgiving, Jet wandered in .... then, on Easter Sunday morning, the cat they call Peeps made it a threesome.
6. Sandra seemed to sense that her partner held the trump ace .... yet she deliberately underbid the hand.
7. No one claims that the red rambling roses are more attractive than the New York Pinks .... I simply state that they are a showier flower.
8. Yupon and Poison Sumac grew on the upper ten acres .... elsewhere over the ranch grew mesquite and huisache.
9. She tried first tape, then glue, and finally staples .... however, Frances' Man in the Moon shadow box fell apart before fifth period.
10. The young wife insisted that air conditioning in that two-room west-side apartment was essential .... her husband called her an extravagant simpleton.
11. If the student lives in Duncan Hall, or Dorms 11, 12, or 13, his laundry problems are solved .... if he lives in Milton Square or close to the Quadrangle, he practices the do-it-yourself system.

12. Bill bought shares in two local banks and spent two weeks fishing in Mexico .... therefore his parents assumed that he could scrape by without further loans from them.
13. Mrs. Anderson embroidered icon after saintly icon .... but she would not part with one of her collection, although they lay yellowing in the trunk of heirlooms in the parlor.
14. Six, seven, and eight come first .... eleven comes somewhat later.

Coordinate Elements in Series

When more than two coordinate elements appear together, they are a series. Any three or more equal grammatical elements can appear in a series—nouns, verbs, participles, noun clauses, prepositional phrases, or any part of a sentence. For instance, this sentence shows verbs in a series:

> Cathy *ran, skipped,* and *jumped.*

Or this one has three noun clauses in a series:

> Lois never stopped to consider *that the weather was not favorable, that the boys did not want to go,* and *that the highways would be too crowded for comfortable travel.*

1. When coordinate elements are used in a series, a comma separates each element from the others. The two sentences just used as examples illustrate this punctuation. It may be diagrammed this way:

(First element)   (Second element)   and   (Third element)
.............................., ..., ...

The comma before *and* between the second and third elements is commonly left out. This practice is acceptable as long as the reader has no chance of assuming that the last two elements are linked together to the exclusion of the first.

2. The coordinate elements in a series must be parallel (that is, the same grammatically). The elements here are italicized:

> Jo did the job *quickly, competently,* and *hardly working at all.*

In this sentence, three adverbs are supposedly in a series; but one element in the series is not an adverb. This can be seen in a diagram.

	(1) quickly
Jo did the job	(2) competently
	and
	(3) hardly working.

The third element will have to be changed to make it parallel with the other two, that is, it must be grammatically the same. This sentence makes that change.

	(1) quickly
Jo did the job	(2) competently
	and
	(3) easily.

Jo did the job quickly, competently, and easily.

Or look at this sentence:

The instructor told them *to study Chapter IV, to make notes on it,* and *that they would have a quiz next period.*

A diagram will expose the elements in this sentence that are not parallel.

	(1) to study Chapter IV
The instructor told them	(2) to make notes on it
	and
	(3) that they would have a
	quiz next period.

The first two elements of the series here are infinitive phrases (that is, *to* plus a verb plus a noun), but the third element is a noun clause (with *that* as the subordinating conjunction, *they* as the subject, and *would have* as the verb). Because these elements are not the same grammatically, the third element must be changed to make it an infinitive phrase starting with *to* plus a verb.

	(1) to study Chapter IV
The instructor told them	(2) to make notes on it
	and
	(3) *to prepare* for a quiz
	next period.

The instructor told them to study Chapter IV, to make notes on it, and to prepare for a quiz next period.

Here is a different one:

Although not many of the class went, those who did found the lecture heavy, profound, and the acoustics in the lecture hall adequate, although not everything could be heard.

This sentence appears to have a series of three. In truth it does not, because it has two subjects—*lecture* and *acoustics*. Look at this sentence in diagram form.

Although not many of the class went,

	(1)	heavy
	(2)	dull
those who did found the lecture		and
	(a)	adequate
	(3)	acoustics
	(b)	not everything could be heard.

Acoustics (a noun) is not parallel with *heavy* and *profound* (adjectives), nor can these three be changed to make them parallel. But the sentence can be improved by making *lecture* parallel with *acoustics* (both nouns).

Although not many of the class went,

			(a)	dull
	(1)	the lecture		
			(b)	heavy
those who did found		and		
			(a)	poor
	(2)	the acoustics		
			(b)	adequate.

Although not many of the class went, those who did found the lecture heavy and dull, and the acoustics in the lecture hall poor but barely adequate.

All coordinate elements in a sentence must be clearly parallel, whether there are more than two elements or only two. Sometimes a fuzzy parallelism will confuse the reader temporarily, as in this sentence:

The lawyer begged that the accused be judged insane and committed to a mental hospital.

Momentary confusion may result here because the reader may want to insert *be judged* before committed, because apparently *insane* and another adjective are being joined by *and*. A diagram illustrates the possible confusion.

The lawyer begged that the accused
    (1) be judged insane
            and
    (2) committed to a mental hospital.

The solution is simple: The parallelism is made clear if *be* is put before *committed*, as well as before *judged*.

The lawyer begged that the accused
    (1) be judged insane
            and
    (2) be committed to a mental hospital.

The lawyer begged that the accused be judged insane and be committed to a mental hospital.

This sentence is similarly confusing:

He said he had read the poetry of Thomas, Spender, and the novels of Updike.

Here the writer has attempted to create a series of three coordinate elements, but there are only two. Look at a diagram of this sentence as the author wrote it.

He said he had read the poetry of
    (1) Thomas
    (2) Spender
            and
    (3) the novels of Updike.

Obviously, *Thomas, Spender,* and *the novels* are not parallel. *Poetry* and *novels* are, however. Then there is a better construction for the sentence.

```
                                        (a)  Thomas
                        (1)  the poetry of
                                        (b)  Spender
He said he had read                  and
                        (2)  the novels of Updike.
```

He said he had read the poetry of Thomas and Spender, and the novels of Updike.

The comma is placed before the second *and* for clarity. Otherwise, the reader might expect the material following Spender to be a third element in a series. The comma specifies that it is not.

Here is another example of faulty parallelism:

His musical career, unlike most students who played in the band, continued after he left high school.

The fault here is one of logic. Careers and students are being compared, but they cannot be compared. It is like attempting to make a comparison between apples and wood splinters; they have nothing in common. So they cannot be made parallel in this way. A diagram of this attempted parallelism looks like this:

```
His musical career
        unlike       continued. . . .
most students
```

This sentence can be made logical and parallel.

```
His musical career
        unlike       continued. . . .
the musical careers of most students
```

Now careers are compared to careers, and the sentence is logically parallel. But a substitute, a pronoun for *career*, is more suitable than repeating the noun so soon after it is first given. The sentence then looks like this:

His musical career, unlike *those* of most students who played in the band, continued after he left high school.

EXERCISE

Correct any nonparallel elements you find in these sentences.

1. He studied the grouping of the stars in their constellations and how close Saturn is to Pluto.

2. The desk had a scratched top, a sticky drawer, and one leg wobbled.

3. Slicing away at the Winesap and whistling as he pared, Eric knew that the first cucumbers were already spoiled on the vine, how he would have to rebuild the chicken roosts tomorrow, and his son had asked him twice to repair his toy truck.

4. He bought a pound each of nails, woodscrews, and a gallon of red paint.

5. Dr. Payne's tests, like all the other professors', were complex, detailed, and offered great difficulty.

6. Since he had already ruined his chances to recover the money and recouping his loss, Ronald shrugged, grinned, and, turning away, sauntered whistling down the hall.

7. Pete was quite slow in discovering that he had no singing voice, could not act, and his personality did not project well.

8. The gold plastic bracelet from the local dime store, added to Ruthie's talent on the dance floor and appreciating the excellent dance band, made the evening a mad memory.

9. Despite his aversion to seafood and liquor, he ate oysters, catfish, and drank beer.

10. Although the house was dark and because he knew the family was out of town, Greg went ahead with his plan to repair the television set in the living room and resetting the loose tiles on the kitchen floor.

SUBORDINATION

In considering matters of sentence structure, *superior* constructions are independent clauses; they carry the main thought of the sentence and are complete in themselves. Words, phrases, and dependent clauses are *inferior*, or subordinate, because they do not consist of a complete thought; they are used most often as modifiers of some part of the independent clause. Sometimes they are used as the subject or verb or complement in an independent clause. The process of subordination, then, is changing what might be stated in an independent clause into an inferior or subordinate construction and attaching it to a part of another independent clause. Consider these two sentences:

> John completed his final examination. Two hours still remained in the examination period.

One of these independent clauses (independent clauses and sentences are the same structurally) can be subordinated to the other and the two combined into one sentence. First, you must decide which idea in the two sentences is the more important one, because it must come in the independent clause. Because the writer put it last, he apparently considers the idea of the second sentence the more important of the two. Then subordinate the first independent clause to the second in one of these ways:

> *When John completed his final examination,* two hours still remained in the period. (Independent clause reduced to a dependent clause. Note that the only difference between an independent and a dependent clause is the presence of a subordinating conjunction, *when* in this sentence, at the beginning of the dependent clause. Other subordinating conjunctions are *while, that, since, although, until, which, who, because, as if, if, when, before.*)

> *Upon completing his final examination,* John discovered that two hours remained in the period. (Independent clause reduced to a prepositional phrase.)

> *Completing his final examination,* John discovered that two hours remained in the period. (Participial phrase)

> *His final examination completed,* John discovered that two hours remained in the period. (An absolute construction)

> John discovered *upon completing his final examination* that two hours remained in the period. (Prepositional phrase)

> John discovered that two hours remained in the period, *although he had already completed the final examination.* (A dependent clause with the subordinating conjunction *although.* The addition of the dependent clause makes the sentence loose in structure.)

Here is a more complicated example:

> [1]Our best quarterback was caught stealing Primitive University's mascot. [2]This happened at the beginning of the football season, and so [3]he was not allowed to play after the first game, [4]thus causing us to lose the championship.

This sentence is written in a primer style; it is a string of independent clauses, except that the main point—We lost the championship—is in a phrase at the close of the sentence. Because it is the most important idea in these sentences, this point should be in an independent clause to give it the most emphasis, whereas the other inferior material should be subordinated. Then, *this* (at 2) and *thus* (at 4) should both be deleted. In this sentence, *this* is a pronoun with vague reference. It does not refer the reader to a single noun, as it should, but to action expressed in the preceding sentence. *Thus* is used as a conjunction. As one of the Group 2 coordinating conjunctions, it joins two independent clauses. But here it is not serving this function; instead, it is joining an independent clause to a phrase. *Thus* can then be deleted without affecting the meaning of the sentence, and there is no structural problem. Here is a revision with the main idea in the independent clause and with other ideas subordinated to it. The ideas are numbered for comparison with the unrevised version.

[4]We lost the championship because our best quarterback, [1]caught [2]at the beginning of the season stealing Primitive University's mascot, [3]was not allowed to play after the first game of the year.

In revising, remember to select the main point in your sentences and subordinate all others to it by casting them in dependent clauses, phrases, or single-word modifiers.

EXERCISE

Make one sentence from each of the following groups of sentences. Cast the main idea in an independent clause and subordinate all other material.

1. It was dark and the night was cold and rainy. Emily started cautiously down the path. It was slippery and clogged by roots and weeds.
2. The chair had one broken leg. It was old and its upholstery was tattered. It collapsed with Pete when he sat in it. A loud noise resulted.
3. The secretary ripped the paper from the typewriter roller. She gave a sharp exclamation and slammed her pencil on the desk.
4. The gringos crowded the Mexican streets. They all appeared overfed, and they were all underdressed.

5. The book lay by the window. The window was open. Wind flipped and tore the book's pages, and they had been soaked with rain.
6. The university rates high scholastically. It has a library of four million volumes. Its teachers are internationally recognized, and its students are the best from quality high schools.
7. The American elk is a relative of the red deer of other continents. Its scientific name is *Cervus canadensis* of the family *Cervidae*. It is occasionally attacked by cougars.
8. They had loved their home. It had three bedrooms, a sun parlor, and impeccably kept gardens. But now the West Church Street School had been built across the street. It housed the first graders who could not be accommodated in the old elementary school.
9. Nancy waltzed proudly around the floor. The hem of her stylish, black-sequined dress had come loose in two places. A lock hung limply from the back of her unswept hairdo. People were tittering. She did not know all this, of course.
10. Jordan was only three and a half when it happened, but he can still remember Uncle Jake shooting the largest elk the state had recorded. The elk stood five feet, nine inches tall and weighed eleven hundred pounds.

SUMMARY EXERCISES

1.

Monte Alban in period IIIb was a nearly incredible enterprise. It occupied not only the top of a large mountain, but also the tops and sides of a whole range of high hills adjoining, a total of some fifteen square miles of urban construction. Human labor may be characterized as cheap under some circumstances, but a man's time is never cheap in a pre-industrial economy, where what he eats has to be produced by hand labor. Except for the possibility of catching more or less rainwater during four or five months of the year, the population of Monte Alban had to drink water carried up the mountain—as much as 1,500 feet—in jars. This alone would be costly; but the quantities of water required in building construction make the location of a large city on this high ridge even more astonishing. In addition, the maintenance of a major religious capital such as Monte Alban would necessarily require the services of thousands of specialists: priests, artists, architects, the apprentices of all these, and many kinds of workmen, including servants for the dignitaries and their families.[2]

[2]John Paddock, "The Cloud People of Monte Alban," *Stanford Today*, October, 1966. Reprinted by permission of *Stanford Today*, Leland Stanford Junior University.

1. What is the pointer in the topic sentence (the first sentence)?

2. What method of paragraph development does the author use to support the topic sentence? Why might you have difficulty deciding which method is used?

3. Does this paragraph have coherence? Is there any point where the coherence might be improved? Why?

4. What is the purpose of *This alone would be costly* and *In addition*?

5. Explain the use of commas in the second sentence.

6. In the third sentence, why is *pre-industrial* hyphenated? Why not write *preindustrial*?

7. Why is a comma used after *circumstances* in the third sentence?

8. Why are dashes used in the fourth sentence?

9. In the fifth sentence, why would an author choose a semicolon rather than a comma?

10. Why is a comma used after *in addition* in the sixth sentence?

11. Explain the punctuation in the last sentence, particularly the use of the colon.

2.

Spacecraft that produce immediate, tangible benefits are a fact of life. Weather satellites continually track weather over the entire earth, and communications satellites relay messages and pictures between continents. Soon there will be a third type of practical spacecraft, another tool to help man understand and control his environment—the natural resources satellite. In its effect on the billions of persons who inhabit this planet, it may be the most important space program yet undertaken.[3]

1. This introductory paragraph skillfully introduces a broad topic and narrows it to a specific thesis statement. What is the broad topic?

2. What means does the author use to narrow the broad topic to one of its parts?

3. What is the specific thesis statement introduced in this paragraph?

4. What would you expect the author to do in the remainder of the paper?

3.

More communications satellites are sure to be launched over Southeast Asia. Comsat is already planning for a second Pacific satellite to be placed in orbit this year. Later, there are plans for an even bigger satellite with a capacity for 1,200 two-way telephone

[3]Louis F. Slee, "Coming: A Natural Resources Satellite," *Electronic Age*, Autumn, 1966. Reprinted by permission of *Electronic Age*, Radio Corporation of America.

circuits or four television channels—five times the capacity of Intelsat II and a lifetime that is two years longer. Nor is that all. Specifications have already been drawn by Comsat for an even more versatile, higher-capacity communications satellite that could accommodate 6,000 to 8,000 two-way telephone circuits, 12 to 20 television circuits, or perhaps a dozen circuits for communication between flying aircraft and ground stations. Even this huge, excess capacity over current needs is not expected to be too great, considering the future communications requirements of the area.[4]

1. What is the topic sentence?
2. What method has the author used to develop the topic sentence?
3. What coherence devices has he used?
4. One number, *five*, is spelled out. The others are not. What is the difference?
5. *Higher-capacity* and *two-way* are hyphenated. Why?
6. Account for the use of a dash before *five times*. Would a comma be as effective here? Why or why not?

4.

Business methodology has changed significantly in the past few years. Rising costs and increasing competition in the postwar era have intensified the profit squeeze in many industries and have encouraged corporate officers to seek improved management methods. Accelerated technical change and more efficient transportation have resulted in a trend to multiplant firms which in turn has intensified the need for improved control. In business management itself, new analytical techniques, developed by economists and systems specialists, have aided in the solution of complex business problems. The final, and perhaps the most important, change has been the development of the electronic computer with its unique capability for processing and analyzing vast quantities of information with phenomenal speed and accuracy.[5]

1. By what method is this paragraph developed?
2. Write an outline of the paragraph, showing major and minor supporting points.

5.

Still, the computer has not operated at the limit of its capacities. Many of the newer and more sophisticated data processing techniques are being applied in market forecasting and analysis. For

[4]Mitchell Levitas, "Communications Boom in Southeast Asia," *Electronic Age*, Autumn, 1966. Reprinted by permission of *Electronic Age*, Radio Corporation of America.

[5]Robert E. Tolles, "The Computer: Management Tool," *Electronic Age*, Autumn, 1966. Reprinted by permission of *Electronic Age*, Radio Corporation of America.

instance, RCA Victor has recently instituted a system for analyzing the results of RCA Record Club sales through advertisements placed in various national publications and through direct-mail solicitation. The information necessary for this analysis was derived from a data bank into which has been placed the names, addresses, and ordering and payments history of all Club members. The system has enabled the Club to arrive at some tentative conclusions on the relative effectiveness of the advertising media and the various types of record offers.[6]

1. The first sentence is not the topic sentence of the paragraph. Which one is?

2. What is the function, then, of the first sentence?

3. What method of development is used in the paragraph?

4. What is the purpose of *for instance* at the beginning of the third sentence? Why is a comma placed after *for instance*?

6.

The cultural fallout from television has been astounding. Critics may, of course, debate the level of musical discrimination shown by an audience that applauds on sight. Yet, the significant thing here is television's incredible ability to increase the awareness of a vast public. The opening of the Lincoln Center for the Performing Arts is a case in point. Some 25.6 million television viewers saw and heard some part of the two-hour concert; in contrast, 2,600 attended the concert that night in Philharmonic Hall. Television attracts the biggest and most heterogeneous audiences in the history of communications. It can attract 16 million people to a program like "Bonanza," and it can interest another 16 million in Leonard Bernstein's "Young People's Concert." Consider the social impact of a program such as Lou Hazam's NBC production, "The Louvre," which drew 15 million viewers when first shown in November, 1965. In 1966 it was run again before an estimated audience of 15 million people. That is a total of 30 million Americans—more Americans than visited the Louvre in Paris since George Washington was President.[7]

1. This paragraph is developed chiefly by reasons supported by illustrations. Outline it using this form:

Topic Sentence: ....

BECAUSE:

  Reason 1: ....

  Supporting Illustration ....

[6]*Ibid.*

[7]Desmond Smith, "The Social Impact of Television," *Electronic Age*, Summer, 1965. Reprinted by permission of *Electronic Age*, Radio Corporation of America.

BECAUSE:

Reason 2 ....

Supporting illustrations:

  A. ....

  B. ....

2. What coherence devices are used in the paragraph?

3. Why is *of course* (second sentence) set off by commas?

4. Why is *yet* (third sentence) followed by a comma? What function does *yet* serve in the sentence?

5. Why is a semicolon used after *concert* (fifth sentence)?

6. Why is a dash used in the last sentence?

7.

The uncanny ability of video to involve the viewer deeply is well known. For example: KQED, a San Francisco educational TV station, ran a half-hour program about Japanese brush painting. Since it was a "how to" program, a young woman producer bought 300 painting kits in anticipation of a moderate viewer response. The station eventually sold a staggering total of 14,000 sets at $3.00 each. And when the H. J. Heinz Company offered a salad recipe book on a single daytime commercial, more than 112,000 viewers wrote in for a copy. When Leonard Bernstein reported the reception the New York Philharmonic-Symphony received on one of its recent tours, he said there was "an explanation other than musicianship to explain the extraordinary enthusiasm" of the audience. "You can't imagine," he said, "how we have been gathered in by audiences that obviously know about us through television." There were places where the audiences stood and cheered for minutes before the orchestra even played a note.[8]

1. What is the topic sentence of this paragraph?

2. What is the pointer in the topic sentence?

3. What basic method of development does the author use in this paragraph?

4. Is this paragraph unified? Does any sentence fail to support the pointer in the topic sentence?

5. What means of achieving coherence are used in this paragraph?

6. Why does the author place a colon after *For example*?

7. Why does he quote *how to*?

8. Why is *half-hour* hyphenated?

9. Why does the author start the quotation, *an explanation other than* . . . , without capitalizing *an*?

[8]*Ibid.*

10. At the end of the Berstein quotation, the period is put inside the final quotation mark. Is this practice correct? Which marks are put inside the quotation marks and which outside?

8.

Though they are not produced in wide-screen Cinemascope, have never won an Oscar, and cannot be viewed on "Saturday Night at the Movies," electronic films are already smash hits in many important sectors of modern electronics technology. Increasingly, they are being "booked" into television equipment, computer logic and memory circuits, two-way communications systems, missile and spacecraft controls, and of course, pocket radios. In fact, if present trends continue, they may yet make the electronics industry the new "film capital" of the world.

As distinguished from photographic film, electronic films are delicate tattoos of electronically active material condensed, for the most part, from hot vapors onto cold, hard, insulating surfaces such as glass. Depending on the materials used and the manner in which they are deposited, such films—many of them 10 times thinner than the shimmering coat of an ordinary soap bubble—may act singly or in combination as whole electronic circuits or simply as components thereof from transistors, diodes, and oscillators to resistors, capacitors, and interconnection paths.[9]

These are beginning paragraphs from a long article. The first is an introductory paragraph, and the second is a paragraph of definition. Together they form the necessary introduction to the article.

1. What point is to be established in the article? What is the specific thesis statement for the article?

2. Is the introductory paragraph a good one? Why or why not?

3. In the second paragraph, is definition by classification used? If so, where is this definition found?

4. The author uses two other methods to make his definition clear. What are they?

5. In the first paragraph, why does the author use quotation marks around *Saturday Night at the Movies*? Why around *booked*? Why *film capital*? Would any of these be just as effective without the quotation marks?

6. In the first paragraph, why are commas placed after *Cinemascope, Oscar,* and *Movies*? Is the comma inside the quotation mark after *Movies* properly placed?

[9]Bruce Shore, "Electronic Films," *Electronic Age*, Summer, 1966. Reprinted by permission of *Electronic Age*, Radio Corporation of America.

7. In the second paragraph, explain the comma after *film*; after *condensed* and *part*; after *cold* and *hard*.

8. Why are dashes used after *films* and *bubble*? Would commas serve just as well here?

9. What coherence devices are employed in these paragraphs?

10. Analyze sentences for suspension of the subject, verb, or complement.

9.

The different international attitudes toward action and violence in children's programs were pointed out when NBC Enterprises co-produced an animated series with Mushi Productions in Japan. It seems the Japanese can comfortably separate reality from fantasy and do not object to a children's program in which death is presented. In one of the co-produced "Astro-Boy" episodes, the story included a highway accident in which at hot-rod driver kills a pedestrian. For syndication in the United States, the plot of the program was softened by skilled translators. Instead of being killed by a hot-rod driver, the pedestrian was slightly hurt in an unavoidable accident. The audience could then identify with the young driver of the automobile and sympathize with both the driver and the pedestrian.[10]

1. What is the topic sentence?

2. What is the pointer in the topic sentence?

3. What is the chief method of developing the topic sentence? What other method is used in combination with it?

4. Can you see any objection to beginning the second sentence with *It seems. . . .*? If so, what might you substitute?

5. Explain the use of a comma after *episodes* in the third sentences, after *United States* in the fourth, and after *driver* in the fifth?

6. Why is *hot-rod* hyphenated?

7. Why is a comma not used before the first *and* in the last sentence?

The next selection is excerpted from an article of about 2500 words. It is, in effect, a five-hundred-word paper within the longer paper, and it establishes one point in support of the thesis of the longer article. Here, in other words, the five-hundred-word paper serves the same function in a 2500-word article as the paragraph does in the shorter paper.

10.

All of this is by way of saying that the computer will eventually have no less impact on engineers and engineering than gunpowder had on archery. It will be registered in several ways.

[10]Al Husted, "American Television Abroad," *Electronic Age*, Autumn, 1966. Reprinted by permission of *Electronic Age*, Radio Corporation of America.

For one, the computer is going to intellectualize the practice of engineering to a degree inconceivable until now. In the past, the engineer has resorted to pencil, slide rule, and T-square to fashion his new designs; a machine shop and mechanical skills to develop his prototypes; and a pilot line to evolve their manufacture. Now, in theory, all but the conception of the idea can be accomplished by computer in tandem with automatic tools. Thus, instead of plotting his design on paper, the engineer will reduce it to a mathematical program. Instead of developing a physical prototype, he will construct a mathematical analogue and let it stand for his prototype. In addition, this analogue will take into account not only engineering matters but technological, operational, economic, and environmental factors that may be pertinent. The computer will then be asked to decide, in effect, whether the design is worth building. Waste and inefficiency in the design process will shrink to a minimum, hopefully, and ill-conceived products will never emerge from the computer.

There will be more to it than this, however. The computer will also make it possible for the engineer to consider the whole context in which his new design is to function. It will compel him consciously or unconsciously to think in systems rather than component terms. A greater emphasis on systems design will be in the inevitable result. More and more, the engineer will conceive the system and let the computer work out the components.

Finally, there is the somewhat imponderable but intriguing matter of the modifications and innovations in design which will stem directly from the man-machine interaction that results when he works with a computer. There is a modern anthropological theory that progress is the result of man's interaction with his own tools. It holds that the evolution of civilization has been and is a great boot-strap operation that has seen man invent tools, which experience then causes him to modify and differentiate until ultimately they inspire the invention of still more tools, which then are modified by experience and lead to yet newer tools, and so on.[11]

1. What is the thesis statement of this selection?

2. What is the topic sentence of the second paragraph?

3. What methods of paragraph development are used in the second paragraph?

4. What point is made in the third paragraph? Do you consider this paragraph to be well-developed? Why or why not?

5. What point is made in the fourth paragraph? How is it established?

6. Note that this selection has no concluding statement because it is part of a longer article. Add a concluding statement.

[11]Bruce Shore, "Computers and Engineers," *Electronic Age*, Winter, 1966/67. Reprinted by permission of *Electronic Age*, Radio Corporation of America.

7. How does the author achieve coherence between paragraphs?

8. What coherence devices does he use within paragraphs?

9. In the second sentence of the second paragraph, the author uses two semicolons. Why has he not used commas here?

10. Wherever commas have been used in this selection, explain their use.

The next selection is also taken from a 2500-word article, but here, in effect, two five-hundred-word papers are used in succession to establish two of the points in support of the article's thesis.

11.

The record of censors is, on the whole, bad. As Mr. Justice Douglas said, in his dissent in the Roth case, "If experience in this field teaches anything, it is that censorship of obscenity has almost always been both irrational and indiscriminate." One need only scan a list of books censored as obscene in the United States in the past few years to make the point. There are several reasons why we can predict similar performances for the future.

It has been suggested that the paranoid personality is drawn to censorship. This is too hard, but the psychology of censorship *is* a curious thing. The demand for censorship does not come from persons who want their own morals protected. Censorship, in the words of Goodwin Watson, "represents the White Soul's Burden." The censorious want to save the rest of us, not by persuasion, but by imposition. They are zealous, self-righteous missionaries in the service of a militant faith. However carefully and temperately a law is drawn its enforcement will come into their intemperate hands. They are the ones who care.

Balance aside, how qualified is the typical censor? The post of censor is not likely to attract the individual with the kind of literary training and ability that will make it possible for him to judge books in the proper context. Few censors are really prepared to do their job well. Milton saw the point clearly in the *Areopagitica*: "If he be of such worth as behoves him, there cannot be a more tedious and unpleasing journey-work, a greater loss of time levied upon his head, than to be the perpetual reader of unchosen books and pamphlets. We may easily see what kind of licensers we are to expect hereafter, either ignorant, imperious and remiss, or basely pecuniary."

But even if he is balanced and qualified the censor can be expected to abuse his office. The function of a censor is, after all, to censor. He has a professional interest in finding things to suppress. His career depends on the record he makes. When in doubt he will err on the side of the angels. The greater outcry would come from his constituency if he let a dirty book slip through than if he suppressed a safe one. The pressure is, inevitably, in the direction of overcensorship.

Since obscenity as a legal term bears no meaning, the operation of censoring laws is bound to be varying, perverse, and unpredictable. One man's sex is another man's obscenity, and there is no objective standard against which to measure. Censors and judges, like the rest of us, lack the ability to apply such terms objectively or consistently. Thus laws and judicial decisions in the obscenity area produce legal uncertainty and social insecurity.

Law enforcement in disregard of individual rights is a major civil liberties problem in the United States. One effect of censorship laws has been to increase the opportunities for this kind of abuse. Policemen, taking advantage of the law's vagueness, can use the threat of prosecution as a means of coercing citizens who are confused about their rights, who wish to avoid the undesirable aspects of prosecution or who are, as so many are, dependent on the tolerance of officials for their continued business existence. Official censorship can easily be used repressively even though the forms of legal procedure are observed, since these cases never come to court.

Censorship laws also provide opportunities for private persons and groups to force their own standards on the community. Some church-derived groups, in particular, have used police pressure and threats of prosecution as weapons against bookdealers, distributors, and publishers, even when the publications in question probably are not legally obscene. This is clearly wrong. The right of such groups to urge their position is unquestioned, but they have no right to abuse the law to achieve their ends. The inherent irrationality and uncertainty of antiobscenity laws make such abuse possible.

The problems created by censorship, although on a smaller scale, are similar to those created for the nation under prohibition. The demand for pornography exists, is substantial, and is met by bootleggers. The law does not successfully limit their activity. It merely determines the channels that activity will follow. Meanwhile the illegality of allegedly obscene publications adds to their glamour, creates a criminal subgroup which exploits them, and otherwise actually magnifies rather than diminishes the problem it is supposed to control.[12]

1. Divide this selection into what amounts to two five-hundred-word papers, each with its own introductory paragraph, thesis statement, and developmental paragraphs.

[12]John Henry Merryman, "The Fear of Books," *Stanford Today*, October, 1966. Reprinted by permission of *Stanford Today*, Leland Stanford Junior University.

2. For each of these two "papers," write down the thesis statement and list under it the three points that support this thesis. If any point is only implied, state it specifically.

3. What methods of paragraph development are used in the developmental paragraphs?

4. What means does the author use to achieve coherence between paragraphs?

5. What means of maintaining coherence are used within paragraphs?

6. Explain the use of all commas and quotation marks in the selection.

Index

Index

A

Active voice, 118–21
Adverbs, 132
Argumentation, 4

C

Classification:
    method of definition, 83–88
Coherence, 48–60
    chronological order, 59
    consistent point of view, 49
    pronoun reference, 55
    related sentence patterns, 54
    repetition of key words, 51
    spatial order, 52
    transition words, 56
Commanding words, 130
Comparison:
    examples of, 97, 98, 99
    method of paragraph
        development, 96
Complement, suspension of, 144
Concluding statement, 6
Content, as a point for
    grading, 106
Contrast:
    examples of, 98
    method of paragraph
        development, 96
Coordinate elements:
    punctuation, 148, 150
    structure in series, 150
Coordination, 147–54
    signal words for, 147, 148

D

Deadwood, 125
Deduction, 6
Definition:
    Aristotelian, 83
    examples of, 89
    extended, 88
    methods of, 83–88
    missteps in, 84–85
Description, 4
Detail, use of, 66–80
Developmental paragraphs,
    6, 66–104
Diction:
    active voice, 118–21
    commanding words, 130
    exhausted phrases, 128
    false words, 130
    "fine" writing, 132
    forcing reader to love it, 129
    hazy words, 133
    listless verbs, 122
    "ly" words, 132
    passive voice, 118–21
    preaching, 130
    stilted wording, 131
    trite words, 127
    vague words, 133
    who and *which,* 124

E

Emphasis, sentence, 139–41
Enumeration, method of
    definition, 86

Example, method of
 definition, 86
Exhausted phrases, 128
Exposition, 3
Extended definition, 88

F

Fact, definition of, 69, 79
False words, 130
"Fine" writing, 132
Forcing reader to love it, 129
Function, method of
 definition, 87

G

General, definition of, 73, 80
Grades on papers, 106

I

Illustration:
 examples, in paragraphs, 92–95
 method of definition, 86
 method of paragraph
  development, 91
Induction, 6
Inference, 71, 80
Introductory paragraph,
 65–66, 79
 position of, 5

J

Judgment, definition of, 70, 80

L

Listless verbs, 122
Loose sentence, 142

M

Mechanics, as point for
 grading, 106

N

Narration, 3, 4

O

Operational method of
 definition, 87
Opinion, 70, 80
Organization, as point for
 grading, 106

P

Paragraph development:
 combination of methods,
  103–104
 comparison, 96
 contrast, 96
 definition, 81
 detail, 68–80
 illustration, 91–95
 reasons, 99–102
Parallelism, 150
Passive voice, 118–19
Periodic-Loose sentence, 143, 145
Periodic sentence, 141–42
Pointer for topic sentence,
 40, 41, 43, 100, 101
Point of view, 30, 49
Preaching, 130
Pronoun reference, 55
Punctuation of coordinate
 elements, 148
Purpose statement, 32–35

R

Reasons:
  examples of, 100–102
  method of paragraph
    development, 99–102
Related sentence patterns, 54

S

Sentences:
  emphasis, 139–40
  loose, 142
  periodic, 139
  periodic-loose, 143, 145
  secondary patterns, 146–56
  simple, 136–41
Series, coordinate, 150
Signal words for coordination,
    147–48
Spatial order, 52
Specific, definition of, 73, 80
Specific details, examples of,
    75–77
Stilted wording, 131
Student papers, analysis of,
    7–9, 11–13, 106–16
Subject:
  choosing, 20
  limiting, 21
  suspending, 143
Subordination, 155–58
Suspension of sentence elements:
  subject, 143
  verb, 144
  complement, 144
Synonym, as method of
    definition, 86

T

Thesis Statement, 79, 80
  definition of, 5
  framing, 23
  position of, 5
  predicate area of, 26–27
  subject area of, 25
Titles for papers, 110
Topic sentence, 80
  definition of, 6
  position of, 6
Transition between
    paragraphs, 67–68
Transition words, 56
  guidelines for using, 58–59
Triteness, 127

U

Unity:
  paragraph, 37–45
  sentence, 138

V

Vague words, 133
Verbs:
  listless, 122
  suspended, 144

W

Who and *which*, 124
Word order, normal, 136